Blessed!

Stories in the Life of a Golf Professional!

by

James F. "Jeff" Burey Jr.

PGA Professional

PUTTER BOY

Also known as "The
Golf Lad" or "The Golf
Boy," the historic symbol
of Pinehurst was sculpted
as a sundial by Lucy
Richards in 1912.

ISBN 978-1-63821-224-9

Printed by Walsworth Publishing Company, Inc. Marceline MO.

Blessed!

Stories in the Life of a Golf Professional!

by

James F. "Jeff" Burey Jr.

PGA Professional

Foreword By:

Tom Watson

Contents

Wolf Creek, Prairie Dunes Kansas & Beyond

FOREWORD

The game of golf is rich with stories from people who play this wonderfully challenging and frustrating game. Their successes and failures make us laugh....and cry. For the passionate golfer, nothing can be more enjoyable, other than hitting that rare dead solid perfect shot, then sitting down and reading the chronologies of golfers who share their stories and their mutual passion for the game. Jeff Burey is one of those golfers and in this book are his life stories.

Jeff's love affair with our game reflects his love of life, family, and friends. Reading his stories in this book we learn about how he started out as a caddie for ABC's great Jim McKay to his continuing serious efforts to teach the fun of playing golf to our young. He has thought outside the box on behalf of our kids as he has come up with unique concepts to attract kids to the game, like his Twin Oaks Wee Links six-hole 150-yard course built on just one acre of land. Kids love it because it's within their abilities. They more easily experience the joy of success in making a birdie or a par which carries a lot of weight in whether they continue to play the game or not.

We all owe a great deal of debt to Jeff for all he has done to expand and enrich the playing of our game, not only with our young but all golfers who have crossed his path.

I hope you find as much enjoyment in reading the stories of his life and golf experiences as I did.

Tom Watson

DEDICATION

To my "Faithful" family

My best friend and beautiful wife Cathy Pritchard Burey

My children (Catherine Greer, Elisabeth Blair,
John "Jed" Edward, 2 sons in law Andrew & Brad,
and my daughter in law Jessica.)

My Nine Grandkids (Owen Baxter, Myra Catherine,
Wade McIver, Rhett Valentine, Foster James, Harris Paul,
Luke Vernon, Peter Bridger, and John Bartholomew.)

My "GOD."

Thank you for being the best family I could ever imagine!

Your unconditional love and support are unbelievable!

I love you all!

INTRODUCTION

"Golf stories in the life of a Golf Professional"

Every encounter and experience matters! How do I handle them? I have never taken my journey for granted and have always tried to make the most for every situation and opportunity.

Some may say, you're lucky and had a lot of good "Breaks!" Others may say "You worked hard and made things happen."

Both those things are probably true, but as I look back on my wonderful journey thru life with the game of golf, the word that always comes to mind is "BLESSED"

I have so much to be thankful for. I've met the most wonderful people, lived in fantastic places, worked at the best clubs, traveled abroad, made great friends, and most of all, have a great life with my beautiful family.

I often say, "My life is like living in a Fairy Tale!"

It's fun to recall and appreciate some interesting, maybe important, sometimes silly moments, and experiences while on this adventure.

By sharing these stories, my hope is you will enjoy the read, ponder your moments, and golf experiences.

I think a look back is always good and this reflection is great medicine for the soul.

This game is said to be a gift from Scotland. I think the game is a gift from "GOD."

Thanks for your love of golf and looking at some stories from the old golf pro in Kansas!

Jeff Burey

Starting Out
Connecticut

I Figured This One Out !

Like thousands of kids in the early 1960s, I delivered newspapers. I grew up in Connecticut, so we had all four seasons. The summers were hot, and the winters could be bitter cold.

I started my deliveries at about four o'clock in the afternoon, which coincidently was usually when the bad weather hit. Winter afternoons would often have a combination of wind, snow, sleet, hail, or ice. Summer afternoons were sometimes 100-degree scorchers. But there was *never* an excuse for not delivering those rags. I delivered papers six days a week. On a good day, I could complete my route in about an hour and a half. On tough days it could take two and a half hours. On Saturdays, I would collect the fees from my neighbors/customers, which *always* took the full two and a half hours. On a great week, I could expect to earn four to six dollars.

After school one day in May, an older brother of a friend asked if I wanted to caddy. I told him I would like to try it, but I had to deliver my papers first. He told me to show up at the pro shop as soon as I could. I got to the club at about 5 pm that same day and the Caddie Master Joe gave me a crash course in the art of looping. He immediately sent me out with a high school kid who carried two bags. I had a single bag to carry and the member I looped for was very helpful and extremely patient with me. We played nine holes in just under two hours and I was paid four dollars plus a fifty-cent tip. I wasn't always the best student, but I could understand this math!

Without a second thought, I sold my paper route the next day and caddied until I was old enough to work on the golf course.

The Norwalk Hour

Our Secret

In the '60s, before turning 16, I would most everyday caddy at Shorehaven Golf Club in Norwalk, Connecticut.

On an autumn afternoon, after school, while in junior high school in hopes of getting a loop and making a few bucks, I rode my bike to the Caddy Yard. The weather wasn't perfect by any means. It was cool, windy, cloudy with a little mist. Six or eight caddies were waiting for work as well. There hadn't been any golfers for a while and time was marching on.

Finally, Joe the caddie master appeared and asked, "who is next to go!" He said "I have a single for 9 holes." I was the last to get there and the least experienced and remember one of the older Double Caddies ask, "Who is It?" Joe said, "It's Mr. McKay" and the reaction of the other caddies surprised me. They all backed off because Jim McKay was an average/ higher handicap player and they all were older, Double Caddies, and wanted 2 bags to carry. I piped up and said, "I'm ready" and got the assignment

Jim McKay was not a big man but a giant in the sports world. He worked for ABC television, hosted the Wide World of Sports, covered the Kentucky Derby, the Indy 500, and golf events on the PGA tour as well as the British Open.

We teed off and I think we were probably the only two people on the front nine. The first four holes played out how I had expected, bogies and double bogies.

We approached the fifth, 200-yard par-three, downhill, valley short of the green and the flagstick and hole in the middle of the putting surface.

I handed Mr. McKay his driver and he said "Jeff. I've never reached this green." He made a good swing squarely striking the ball, launching that driver and the ball landed in the valley. The ball bounced twice, rolled on to the green, and into the hole for an Ace! I had witnessed my first hole in one and was excited, to say the least. I think McKay was shocked and asked me "Jeff, did that go in the hole?" Beside myself, I said, "Yes Sir!" He was quiet for a minute and then said to me "Jeff, you know we can't tell anyone because no one will believe us. I'm not a good enough golfer to have even reached that green and done that!"

Jim McKay

The last four holes were like the first four, bogies, and doubles. He paid me and added a nice tip and said, "Remember our secret." I headed home for dinner

Fast forward 12-14 years later and I am the Head Golf Professional at Pinehurst. We play host to the Colgate Hall of Fame Classic. The tournament is televised by ABC and Jim McKay is the anchor for the broadcast. Big stuff, biggest purse on the PGA tour, Goodyear blimp, Nicklaus, Watson, Floyd, Palmer, and Miller, etc.

I'm in my office, receive a phone call and it's Jim McKay. He asks if I would meet him at the Pinehurst hotel and have time for a coke. I said, "I'll be right over!" I had not seen him since that 9-hole afternoon.

Our meeting at the hotel wasn't very long but was one I'll never forget. He complimented me on my golf career, and I expressed how well he had handled the crises at the Munich Olympics.

Jim McKay asked me lots of questions about Pinehurst history, #2 course, and a variety of things, but the question of questions was, "Do you remember, and did you ever tell anyone our secret?"

I said, "Wow, I told everyone, caddies, the Pro, caddy master, my mom, dad, Uncle Lou, and more!"

He said, "What did they say?"

I said, "Nobody believed me!"

Jim McKay was right!

Inspiration, Motivation, and Grace

Talent is an amazing gift and it is unbelievable to witness it up close! God given talent nurtured correctly can lead to heights almost unimaginable!

I grew up in the south "Southern Connecticut" (Norwalk) and was surrounded by talent.

Two incredibly gifted athletes were Paul Gerken and Calvin Murphy!

Paul was one year younger and Murph one year older than me. These two are Norwalk High School legends!

My neighbor and good friend growing up was Paul Gerken. Paul at 14 was the number one junior tennis player in New England, for the 16-year old and under-age division. Paul won three consecutive Connecticut state high school championships and had a stellar collegiate career at Stanford and later Trinity University in San Antonio Texas. He was named an All American at both universities! As a professional Gerken competed until 1977. Playing singles and doubles, Paul competed in the French Open, Wimbledon, and 8 times in the US Open. Talent!

Another amazing athlete was Calvin Murphy! Murph played basketball and excelled at all levels. At Norwalk High School he played three years and as a "senior", in 1966, led the team to the Connecticut State championship. Murphy considered the greatest high school player in the history of New England, averaged over 40 points a game in his senior year! At Niagara University he had an outstanding career and was named to the NCAA Division 1 All American Team. Hall of Famer and NBA AllStar, Calvin Murphy played 13 seasons with the NBA's San Diego/ Houston Rockets. At five feet nine inches he was considered the "Mighty Mite." Talent!

Golf was my life as a teenager and as a caddie, I always preferred looping for the best and most talented golfers. Shorehaven Golf Club in Norwalk had one of the very best amateur golfers in

Jerry Courville. Courville, a real gentleman, had a great game and tremendous tournament record. He won the Connecticut State Amateur and Open. His six victories in nine years competing in the New York Metropolitan Golf Association "Ike" Stroke Play Championship was an incredible feat. He had two victories in the MGA amateur and one in the MGA Open. Winning the Travis Memorial at Garden City Golf Club, the Northeast Amateur and a runner-up finish in the

Jerry Courville

1974 USGA Amateur also highlighted Courville's brilliant career.

Caddying for or being a caddie in the group with Jerry Courville was always my favorite experience. I learned so much about golf course management, the pace of play, patience, using creativity, respecting others, being competitive, and understanding the rules of etiquette! These were all kinds of Life lessons.

The first time I ever carried double was a late summer afternoon. Jerry Courville had invited his very good friend, Dick Siderowf, to play and I was assigned the job to loop the nine holes for the twosome. Wow! I was excited!

Shorehaven Golf Club

Dick Siderowf

I had never met Dick Siderowf but knew a little about his stellar golf history. Siderowf's golf career spanned the world! He was a dominant player in the northeast, won the Azalea Amateur, Canadian Amateur, and two British Amateurs. He played on four winning Walker Cup teams and captained a fifth. More talent!

That afternoon Jerry Courville and Dick Siderowf decided to play the back nine holes and I was going to carry double, watch these two great players compete, and get paid for it! On the tee with my heart racing, I handed them their drivers. Two solid drives and we were off!

I managed to do okay on holes 10, 11, and, 12 and their play was spectacular. A par 4 and a birdie at the 10th, two birdies at the par-five 11th, a par 5 and another birdie on 12. I am loving this!

Hole 13 is a long par three! Courville hits his tee shot in the right greenside bunker and Siderowf's ball ends up on the front fringe. I'm a little panicked! My mind is racing with thoughts: Sand wedge for Courville! Is Siderowf going to chip or putt? Where is the bunker rake? Do I need to pull the flagstick? Where do I drop the bags? What club does Siderowf want? I need to pull Courville's putter. I'm overwhelmed and my brain is mush! Watching as Courville is about to play his "bunker" shot, I'm backing up very slowly, and my right heel plants Siderowf's ball, embedding it in the fringe. What do I do now? I'm wishing I could just run and hide! I was so embarrassed!

I then witnessed true "Grace" firsthand!

Jerry Courville came out of the bunker, looked at the top of Siderowf's buried ball, looked at Dick Siderowf, and looked at me! Expecting the worst, Courville just smiled and I think Siderowf might have just laughed! It all worked out! They both knew I was trying my very best and they could have done nothing to make me feel any worse.

We finished that 9-hole round, just before dark! I had learned another life lesson; it was the gift of "Grace."

In March of 1966, a highly motivated Calvin Murphy and I combined for 61 points in that Connecticut State High School Championship basketball game! With 9 seconds left in the game, I snagged a rebound and made the outlet pass! Racing down the court, I graciously received a perfect pass from Calvin! In stride, I make what should be an easy left-handed layup with my right hand! The buzzer sounds and I had scored the final 2 points. "The Murph" had scored the other 59!

State Championship final: Norwalk 93, South Catholic 76

I love to witness the talent and will always appreciate the effort! Paul Gerken, Dick Siderowf, Jerry Courville, and Calvin Murphy inspired me and to this day motivate me to try my best!

Mom Often Said:

"Always look the people you meet in the eye!"

Delores Putnam Burey, my mom, was a special lady! She was my biggest supporter! I will always appreciate her wisdom, encouragement, patience, and her love.

Connecticut in the Fall season is spectacular. The New England autumn colors will take your breath away!

I grew up in Norwalk Connecticut, 45 miles from New York City (Empire State Building). You might imagine Norwalk would resemble the Big city, but it didn't at all. Norwalk was a fabulous place to grow up. This southern New England community had almost everything. The town had great schools, wonderful churches, parks, Long Island Sound, beaches, and so many fantastic people.

Probably, besides home, my favorite place was the Shorehaven Golf Club. As an 11 or 12-year-old I would explore the private golf club's property, hunting for golf balls, fishing the ponds, climbing trees, searching for reptiles (frogs and turtles), and watching golfers play.

I loved to play golf and in our yard, even made a two-hole mini-course with tomato cans in the ground for the holes. Our lawn was worn ragged and not very attractive. When a neighbor would comment my mom would politely say "I'm raising kids, not grass!"

At 13, I started caddying, some thought, to make money. But for me, the main reason for caddying was that caddies could play the golf course on Mondays. The clubhouse, course, and most facilities were closed to members and I lived for Mondays. I very rarely missed the opportunity to play on those days.

Shorehaven had a special arrangement with nearby Birchwood Country Club in Westport about 3 miles away. If Monday

Birchwood Country Club

maintenance closed the club to members play, caddies from the closed club could play the other. What a great idea! Reciprocity for caddies!

One October Monday, Shorehaven was closed for maintenance and arrangements had been made for me to play Birchwood after school. I was now a sophomore in high school and the autumn days were nearly perfect. Birchwood is a beautifully conditioned 9-hole course and all day long my mind was focused on my golf to be played that afternoon.

School finally ended, I raced home, put golf shoes in my golf bag, clubs on my shoulder, jumped on my bike, and was off to Birchwood. At the club, I didn't see anyone and went to the putting green and hit a few putts. As I headed to the first tee a gentleman approached and asked if I was alone and if he might join me. I said, "sure" and off we went. Nine holes complete and darkness closing in, back on my bike and home for dinner.

At home my mom had dinner in the oven, my dad was working, my brother and sister had eaten. Mom sat down and while I ate, asked me a few questions: "How did you play?" "Pretty well, shot

38 on a good golf course." "Did you play alone?" "No, played with a nice guy!" "What was he like?" "Not a great golfer, but fun to play with." I said, "Mom his eyes were as blue as any I have ever seen!" "Did he introduce himself?" "Yes, he said his name was Paul and I don't remember his last name! He kept score and I have the scorecard in my golf bag," I retrieved the card from my bag and gave it to her. Mom opened the card that was signed with the name Paul Newman. My mom was speechless and couldn't believe her eyes! She said: "Jeff you played with Paul Newman." I had no clue.

Mom has been gone for quite a while now and I sometimes wonder where she put that scorecard. She was always reading, and my guess is it's a bookmark in a book somewhere in a bookcase.

Since that October day, Paul Newman had a superfan in me! I think I've seen all his movies but still have never seen blue eyes like those that day at Birchwood.

Paul Newman in action

Join the Navy and
See the World!

To say the least, the mid to late '60s were a very interesting time, and they had a tremendous impact on my life. I graduated high school in 1967 and was lost as to what was next for me. Golf had been my focus all through school, from the fifth grade on. Although I did play varsity basketball, golf was my passion and I was addicted to the game. I played every junior golf event available, 3 years of high school golf, and spent almost all my time practicing and even working on the grounds crew at our local private golf club to allow me a place to play. As a student, I was average at best and had made no plans for continuing my education after high school. Encouraged by my basketball and golf coaches, I applied and was accepted at Central Connecticut State College. Shortly after arriving I knew I was in the wrong place. I left school after the first semester and went back to work at my hometown golf course.

1968 with the Viet Nam war boiling and having won the Draft Lottery I knew it was time to consider my military options. I knew that being drafted was almost certain and the options offered by the Navy and Air Force seemed to be the way to go. I enlisted in the Navy and had made an unbelievably positive move. My life and future were about to change big time. I was about to learn a trade, take responsibility, learn focus, gain confidence, learn to multitask, and see the world! Be mindful I grew up in Connecticut and the farthest from home for me was Allentown Pennsylvania (150 miles), I was determined to make the most of the experience and grow as a person.

I served 4 years 7 months and 1 day. After completing my navy schooling, I served on the USS America (aircraft carrier), USS Laffey (WW2 Destroyer), and the USS Brunswick (Ocean-going salvage tug).

USS America CVA 66

USS Laffey DD 724

USS Brunswick ATS 3

Golf was still the focus of my time off and I wanted to, at the very least, maintain my golf skills.

After completing basic training, I was able to mix my golf goals with the service goals. While in navy schools I played golf in Illinois, Maryland, Virginia, Connecticut, and Florida, On off days while on the America and Laffey in Portsmouth Va. and Norfolk Va. respectively, I would play Chandler Harper's Bide A Wee, Elizabeth Manor, Little Creek, Oceana Naval Air Station as well as any club that would have me.

I loved to practice, enjoyed the games, and the competition at Oceana Naval Air Station. I spent most of my free time there.

The major portion of my sea time was spent while on board the Laffey. We went to the Caribbean twice and one Mediterranean cruise. Because of my job and having access to storage under the deck (floor) plates in my workspace I was able to stow my golf clubs and two sets of civilian golf clothes as well as my golf shoes. On my first "Springboard" Caribbean trip, I was able to play at San Juan Naval Station, Roosevelt Roads Naval Station, Dorado Beach, and El

Conquistador in Puerto Rico. We also played in Jamaica, St. Croix, but the most interesting place had to be "Gitmo" Guantanamo Bay, Cuba. The golf course had excellent greens, but the fairways and tees were bare dirt. Fidel Castro had cut off water to the base and the United States had constructed a desalinization facility that produced freshwater to supply for the base, hence water for greens only. We carried and played our shots from tee to green by placing a coco doormat under the ball. I can't remember a score but will never forget the experience.

The Mediterranean experience was unbelievable. I did see numerous historic sights and many cultures but also focused on my golf opportunities. After crossing the Atlantic and entering the Med our first port of call was Beleau, France. Located midway between Nice, France, and Monte Carlo, three of us sailors took a cab to the Monte Carlo Golf Club. We played 36 holes. The drive up to the club and all the hairpin curves made for some memories. You could see the beautiful and spectacular French Riviera from the course. The contrast in color, bright blue sky, all the different greens, the pure white clouds, and brilliance of the blue Mediterranean waters. I felt rich!

We sailed next to Sardinia and then on to Naples, Italy. We played a very nice course (27 holes) at an air force base 30 minutes or so from the ship. Back to sea for a while, we did navy stuff and then caught a bad break (?). We had a problem with a fire control computer and had to spend a week in Pyreis (Athens), Greece. I discovered a fantastic course (Glyfada) located very near the Athens airport. I played three times that week. From Athens, we sailed the Aegean Sea and to Turkey. No golf there. On to Rhodes, Greece, and great history but no golf. Next to Valletta, Malta where we played the Royal Malta Golf Club. I had my first experience with sand greens. From Malta, it was off to Brendesi, Italy, and back to Naples for one last round of golf and a day trip to Rome. Our next port of call was Palma de Majorca, Spain with no golf but there was anticipation to begin our trip across the Atlantic and back to Norfolk, Virginia. The total Mediterranean cruise was approximately nine months, I pulled my weight with the navy stuff, but playing 13 rounds of golf was what I remember most fondly.

Back in Norfolk/Portsmouth for reconditioning, "R and R" and preparation for a second "Springboard" to the Caribbean. This period allowed for a lot of golf.

As my Navy career neared an end, I knew that the golf business was in my future. I had learned of the PGA apprentice program and had set clear goals for myself. As it turned out the most fun and rewarding part of my Navy experience was about to begin. I had expected to spend the last couple of months in the navy in one of the east coast ports, when my orders came, to my surprise, I was to be transferred to Lowestoft, England, and would be on the commissioning crew (five of us) of a salvage ocean-going tug. The USS Brunswick was the third of its class and was in the final stages of construction. Our job was to work with the shipyard and construction contractor and to verify the ship was constructed to our specifications and eventually train the balance of the crew (approximately 90) who were being assembled in Virginia. My job was an 8-4 Monday-Friday job, and although quite demanding did permit me more time than I had ever had to work on my golf game and play. The first place I visited after our housing was in place was the Lowestoft Golf Club, I sought out the club secretary, and after a brief interview, he invited me to play and hence extended me a temporary membership. The people I met and the golf experiences are almost unimaginable for a person who still has a terminal case of golf disease. I played golf all over England and some in Scotland. I played in weekend competitions, partnering with a lady from the Lowestoft Club. The foursome format was new to me, but I adjusted quite quickly to alternate shot golf and we were very competitive.

Two of the highlights of my tour in the UK were my day trip to Woodall Spa in Lincolnshire, England (Tony Jacklin's home course), and my two trips to Scotland. While in Immingham, England, I took a train and rode a bus, to Jacklin's club and played all day. Great weather, wonderful course and a couple of nice members to be paired with. I played very well and was pleased which wasn't the case most times. I made two trips to Scotland. The first on a high-speed train from London to Edinburgh and the second on a Navy mail plane from Mendenhall Air Base to Prestwick. I went to St. Andrew's in hopes of playing the Old Course but didn't realize the

Old course was closed on Sundays, but I walked the course and did play the New Course.

We sailed the Tug across the Atlantic with the British Merchant Navy in charge. We met our crew, commissioned the Brunswick in Portsmouth, Virginia and I was discharged shortly thereafter. Out of the Navy and into the golf business.

Saint Andrews Scotland trip while in the navy!

Bide A Wee

"You don't stop playing golf because you grow old, you grow old when you stop playing golf!"

This was the wording on an entrance sign as you entered Chandler Harper's Bide A Wee golf club in Portsmouth Virginia. Mr. Harper and his club professional, Jimmy Stewart, looked after a young sailor stationed on the aircraft carrier "USS America" in dry dock at the Portsmouth Naval shipyard in 1969.

Bide A Wee, Portsmouth Virginia

My Interview

"You will probably never get rich, but you will live like you are!"

It was the Spring of 1973; I had spent almost five years in the US Navy and was beginning a career in golf. I wanted to play, teach, and be the best golf professional I could be! I had known for 3 or 4 years prior that's what I wanted.

The Navy had been good for me. I had responsibility, gained confidence, and grew up! I played golf my entire Navy time except for the time in basic training.

My plan, even before leaving the navy was to work with either one of two golf professionals. Mike Krak at Wee Burn Country Club in Darien Ct or Claude Harmon at Winged Foot in Mamaroneck NY. There was one minor obstacle, neither Krak nor Harmon knew who Jeff Burey was. I felt these two men were the best at what they did and having either as a mentor was what I wanted and needed.

Mike was a fine player, excellent teacher, and growing up nearby I often read of his tournament successes. We played our high school conference championship three years at his club. When I was in high school, I heard him speak at our local golf association meeting in my hometown. Mike always had outstanding assistant golf professionals and launched them into great careers. I respected Mike Krak before really knowing him.

Claude Harmon, whose career is legendary, was my other option to approach, and as a player, teacher, and mentor of young golf professionals, Mr. Harmon was the premier guy!

I chose to approach Mike Krak and Wee Burn first because it was closer to my home. The day I showed up at Wee Burn was one I will always remember. I had a plan but wasn't very prepared. I showed up unannounced, nervous, in my only nice civilian clothes (I was only two days out of the navy).

My meeting with Mike went something like this:

"Hi, I'm, Jeff Burey and would like to work here with you and enter the PGA apprentice program!"

Mike said "Do you have your Resume? I said to myself "What is a resume?" I told him I had just gotten out of the navy the day before yesterday. Mike told me he had his staff in place but asked me to write my name and phone number down. I picked the pen up, feeling I had blown my chances, handshaking, scribbled my name and number. I got in my car, sat there a few minutes, reflected again on how I had blown it, and began to think how I would approach Claude Harmon tomorrow.

I went home to mom and dad's house and was considering my next move.

The phone rang. It was the golf professional Vinnie Grillo at our local public course. Vinnie asked me "Did you go to Wee Burn and try to get a job with Mike Krak?" I told him "yes, but it hadn't gone very well." He said Mike had called him and he thought I would hear back from him and I did! Mike asked if I would meet him the following morning at Wee Burn and I said I would be there.

With Mike Krak Wee Burn Country Club

My second time meeting with Mike was memorable. He asked about my goals, my playing ability, and my entire background. He watched me hit balls (nervous, caddie grip) I know I expressed that I would do anything to start with him at Wee Burn and become a PGA apprentice. I was hired as a bag room assistant and had the responsibility of overseeing the practice range.

I'll never forget my first day! Mike called me into his office and told me, "Welcome, Jeff you are now in a business you will probably never get rich, but you will live like you are."

My 40 plus year golf career and life have been an unbelievable experience. The friendships, relationships, opportunities, and memories are priceless.

I am so thankful I went to Wee Burn that morning in 1973!

Thank you, Mike Krak,

Surprise Meeting the "King!"

My first year in the golf business was as fun and educational as you could imagine. I was at Wee Burn Country Club in Darien, Connecticut, and working with PGA professional Mike Krak. I was like a sponge soaking up water, watching and being coached by Mike, he could do it all. He could really play, was a Master teaching professional, outstanding manager, and had a passion for club design. Mike seemed to know everyone in the golf industry and he was magnetic.

One morning, not sure, whether it was the week of the Westchester Classic or the Greater Hartford Open, but I know it was a Tuesday because it was Ladies Day. The other assistant and I had just started the ladies with a Shotgun start and I was headed back to the Bag storage room/ club repair shop. I noticed Mike had one of his sand wedges in the vice and was filing the bounce (sole). Another man with his back to me was intensely watching Mike work. As I got a little closer the man turned around and to my surprise, it was The King Arnold Palmer. I think I might have been in shock with Arnie standing 4 feet from me! My tongue was tied, and I have no clue as to what I said. Mike then introduced me to him and then I went back to whatever I was on my way to do. Mike and Arnie again turned their focus to that sand wedge, the file, and the vice.

Jeff Burey and Arnold Palmer 1978

Mike later told me many stories about growing up in West Virginia and his long friendship with Arnold Palmer from nearby, Latrobe, Pennsylvania just across the river. Mike had been an Air Force pilot and on occasion would fly with Arnold.

Later in my career at Pinehurst, I would see Mr. Palmer and he was always, just as you might imagine, a genuine gentleman. I'm not sure he remembered meeting me back in the early '70s, but he always remembered my mentor Mike.

The 16th at Wee Burn, Darien, Connecticut

GOLF

Golf is a science, the study of a lifetime, in which you may exhaust yourself but never your subject. It is a contest, a duel or a mêlée, calling for skill, courage, strategy and self-control. It is a test of temper, a trial of honour, a revealer of character. It affords a chance to play the man and act the gentleman. It means going into God's out-of-doors, getting close to nature, fresh air, exercise, a sweeping away of mental cobwebs, genuine recreation of tired tissues. It is a cure for care, an antidote to worry. It includes companionship with friends, social intercourse, opportunities for courtesy, kindliness and generosity to an opponent. It promotes not only physical health, but moral force.

DAVID R. FORGAN. 1899

John's Island

Florida

Slammin' Sammy

In March of 1973, I started my golf career at Wee Burn Country Club in Darien and later John's Island Club in Vero Beach. As an apprentice PGA golf professional, I had the best of two worlds! The summer season in Connecticut and winters in Florida. What could be better?

I worked with two fantastic golf professionals! Mike Krak in the north and Lou Miller in the south, both great role models, encouragers, and the best mentors.

Mike Krak was the pros' pro! He was recognized as one of the best golf instructors and players as well as an avid student of the game. Mike would use professional golfers swing photos to give his students a visual during or after a lesson. Mike had great photos of Ben Hogan, Sam Snead, and many others.

Like most young professionals I wanted to learn as much as I could to help me communicate as a teaching pro and improve my own swing/ game.

I was reading Ben Hogans' book Five Lessons and I think I was driving Mike crazy with questions. His patience with me was sure appreciated. I remember asking who he thought had the best golf swing? Expecting him to say, Hogan, he without hesitation, said Sam Snead.

Mike's case for Snead was the simplicity, tension-free swing, balance, and repeatability. I knew how much Mike Krak respected Hogan's work ethic and focus on fundamentals, but Snead was his pick.

1951 Ryder Cup Pinehurst

I had seen Samuel Jackson Snead at the Westchester Classic in the late '60s, but I had not seen him up close.

I would later, on two occasions, have the opportunity to meet and spend some time with Sam Snead!

The first-time meeting Snead was in Boynton Beach Florida. Two fellow golf pros from John's Island and I had arranged to play Pine Tree Golf Club. Driving the entrance, into this beautiful club we noticed a caddie shagging balls for a golfer with the smoothest swing I'd ever seen. Golf professional Tom Wilcox said, "that's Sam Snead!"

At the golf shop checking in, we confirmed, with the golf professional, Nelson Long, our tee time and that it was indeed was Sam Snead practicing. One of us asked Nelson if he thought Snead would mind if we watched him. Nelson gave us the okay! Mr. Snead was gracious, friendly, said "yes" and I will never forget what he demonstrated. He said, "Boys watch this." He was hitting wedges

110 yards with his caddie not moving, catching the balls on one bounce. He switched to a nine iron and with a full swing hit the shot 110 yards, one bounce to the caddie. He then hit 8 and 7 irons with full swings 110 yards, again with one bounce to the caddie. He said: "7 iron is as low as I can go boys." We played our 18 holes and all I could think about was what Sam Snead had demonstrated. Four

different clubs, full swings, same distance, and caddie never having to move. Wow!

The second time I met Sam Snead was at Pinehurst. I had joined the Pinehurst staff and moved to North Carolina.

Tom Fazio and his team had been hired to change the grass (Bent to Bermuda) on the greens of Pinehurst Number Two. Also, the plan was to restore the green complexes to what Donald Ross had in the late forties and early fifties.

Since Sam Snead had played "Number Two" so often and he was the playing Captain of the 1951 Ryder Cup team at Pinehurst, his feedback would be very helpful with this project. He was asked to tour the 18 holes and provide his thoughts as to how the green complexes had evolved since nearly 30 years had passed.

Being on the Professional Staff, I was privileged to be assigned to drive Sam Snead for 18 holes and record his recollections. I had a clipboard and a notepad ready to fill with notes of his hole by hole thoughts. His memory was crystal clear and easy to record. I think we spent a couple of hours recording Snead's memories of all the 18 holes.

The extra fun part of the task was listening to the stories of his experiences competing on the Donald Ross masterpiece "Number Two." What a privilege!

I remember reading where Sam said: "The three things I fear most in golf are lightning, Ben Hogan, and a downhill putt." I'm not sure he was at all fearful of anything.

Sam Snead a super legend in golf! He won 82 official PGA Tour events, over 140 tournaments world-wide, and won 7 majors (3 Masters, 3 PGA's, and 1 British Open). In 1974 Snead was elected to the World Golf Hall of Fame in Pinehurst.

Mike Krak may have been right!

A Guy Named Bill!

"Part One"

In January of 1973, as a 24-year-old, I was working as an apprentice PGA professional at John's Island Club. Johns Island is in Vero Beach Florida and was a beautiful place to be. Vero was my winter home and I can't imagine any better place to work, spend the winter, and refine your golf game.

John's Island had the Pete Dye-designed South course and the North, another Dye course, was in the final stages of construction.

Practicing and playing was a daily part of the young professionals on staff for the winter. I couldn't understand why any young, single, golf professional from up in the cold wouldn't come to the sunny south for the winter. I felt like this might be heaven.

One late afternoon, after a practice session, I decided to take my golf cart and take a tour of the North course. From a distance, I noticed work being done in the water hazard in front of the Par 3 16th hole. A couple of young guys were installing vertical railroad ties just in front of the green. (Pete Dye Trademark). Interested, being me, I said "hi" and introduced myself. One of the guys was a guy named Bill. Bill Coore was working with the legendary Pete Dye and his team. Bill liked to play golf and had played on the Wake Forest golf team. We didn't see a whole lot of each other after that first meeting, but Bill and I did play golf at least once. I later learned he was from North Carolina and in 1968 had graduated from Wake Forest, where he studied, of all things, "Classical Greek",

Bill began his career in the golf design and construction business working with Dye in 1972.

The story gets fun from here. In February of 1977, I begin my tenure at Pinehurst Resort and Country club. I met and got to know a fabulous man, who is an excellent player and Pinehurst member. Stuart Kennedy happens to be a very close friend of this guy Bill Coore, who I had met in Florida. Stuart and Bill loved Pinehurst.

Bill almost always shares his respect for the incredible work of Donald Ross,

Stuart Kennedy arranges a trip to Casa de Campo (Dominican Republic) for the International Pro-Am Golf Tournament. I'm on Stuart's team and Bill Coore on another. Beautiful trip, perfect weather, two fantastic Pete Dye courses, relaxing and great fellowship. By now I've figured out this Bill Coore guy is special!

February of 1981, I have just started my job as GM /Golf Director at Wolf Creek in Olathe Kansas. I receive a call and it's Bill Coore. He is in Texas and has routed a second nine holes at a club in Rockport. He invites me to come down from Kansas City to see it. I was thrilled to be asked and said how about Monday (my day off). I booked an early, Southwest flight to Corpus Christi for a day trip. Bill picked me up at the airport and to Rockport we went. What a fantastic trip! Bill painted pictures with his words, as he described his plans. I felt like I was back in school and had the best teacher.

Many years, in December, we made golf trips from Wolf Creek to Houston. I would set us up to play 3-4 courses and we would always include a day trip to Waterwood National in Huntsville. Bill was living there, managing the course, and was always a gracious host. Bill was continually doing a golf course project and often on a machine creating something special.

Bill Coore

In 1986 Bill Coore partnered with Ben Crenshaw forming Coore and Crenshaw Inc. Bill and Ben, a perfect match, shared their love of golf architecture, respect for the great designers (Ross, Maxwell, Mackenzie, Tillinghast, and Macdonald), and philosophy of fitting their courses to the site. I think every piece of raw land rejoiced when Coore and Crenshaw formed their partnership

Bill and I had limited contact for the next 5-7 years, although he was working with the folks at Prairie Dunes in Hutchinson Kansas.

Oh, boy was that all about to change in 1994!

Grow in Sand Hills Hole #8

Moe and More!

January 2nd 1974 I arrived in Vero Beach Florida, to begin my winter job at the John's Island Club. I had spent the 1973 season in Connecticut at Wee Burn Country Club as a first-year PGA apprentice.

The east coast of Florida in January was spectacular. I had left the cold, cloudy, grey, and windy New England in December. The Gulf Stream is closest to the Florida coast in Vero Beach and often Vero is the warmest spot in Florida on winter days. The blue sky, green foliage, brilliant ocean, and intercoastal blue water can take your breath away, it is so beautiful. The city motto of Vero Beach is "Where the tropics begin."

John's Island Golf Director Lou Miller had put together a great group of young, highly motivated, apprentice golf professionals. I was the last to be hired and thrilled to be a part of this group.

Miller's staff was intentionally large because our work schedule would only be 30-40 hours a week. In many ways, for us, it was like being on vacation. We could practice and play almost every day and on some "off" days we would play other east coast Florida courses or call ahead, get permission, and go watch some of the best teachers at work. We watched Bob Toski, Davis Love Jr., Jim Flick, Hank Johnson, John Jacobs, Peter Kostis, and Jack Grout.

My first good friend at John's Island was David Liddle. David had grown up in western Pennsylvania (Sewickley Heights), was my age, an apprentice pro, but unlike most of us was married and lived in Vero Beach year-round. David and his wife made me feel welcome and at home from day one and would often invite me for dinner at their house

David and I made a few of the off day trips together and we always had a good experience and usually learned something special.

One of us heard that a guy named Moe, a legendary Canadian was practicing near Melbourne Florida just north of Vero. I think it was Palm Harbour, so we decided we would go see this mystery man. Of all the golf things we did that winter, this trip might have been the most fun and entertaining.

President Gerald Ford and David Liddle

We spent the day watching Moe Norman practice and David interviewed him. Maybe the most interesting thing was to hear Moe's commentary. He would repeat his answers, "I'm closest to Hogan, closest to Hogan", or 'Straight nearly perfect, nearly."

Moe had freakish talent, callused hands, and could hit balls all day. His ball-striking was pure and his accuracy beyond belief. He could put fifty 4 irons in a pattern the size of a beach blanket. His impact position was nearly perfect. Wow!

1974 winter was special, and I'll never forget that day with Moe and my friend David Liddle.

Back story, David Liddle introduced me to my wife Cathy in January of 1977, and we were married on July 19th, 1978.

John's Island Hole #17 North

You Aren't Winning This Hole!

John's Island Club in Vero Beach, Florida is one of the nicest places to live or visit in the country. For most residents, Johns Island is a winter home. The complex is located between the inter-coastal and the Atlantic Ocean on highway A1A just north of Vero. Besides having the ocean and wonderful amenities, the club has three wonderful courses, the first two designed by Pete Dye.

I became a member of the winter golf staff in 1974.

The first course, the South, had been completed and the North course was being built. I had the privilege of playing almost every evening,

Lou Miller, the club's golf director, put together, one of the finest golf professional staffs. Most of the young apprentice golf professionals had Northern summer season jobs, working at some of the most prestigious country clubs in America. These folks were talented and understood the basics of the business. They all were very smart, good instructors, excellent players, could plan and organize golf events, merchandise, had great people skills, and were also very very competitive. To this day I'm thankful that somehow, I had become a part of that team.

One member of our staff was William J. Mallon "Bill" from Framingham, Massachusetts. Bill was not a professional and was in

Dr. William J "Bill" Mallon

his mid 20's. Being a New Englander myself, I knew of Bill and his very successful junior and amateur career. Bill graduated magna cum laude from Duke University with an A.B. in math and physics. At Duke, Bill also had an outstanding golf career and was twice named All-American. He won over 40 amateur tournaments and Bill had come to work at John's Island in 1974 and was there to hone his game.

HOLE	1	2	3	4	5	6	7	8	9	OUT		10	11	12	13	14	15	16	17	18	IN	TOT	HCP	NET
TOURNAMENT	381	414	441	186	376	387	184	530	348	3247	P	401	489	159	376	506	434	395	158	346	3264	6511		
BACK *Back/Middle*	363	405	417	178	359	370	178	505	340	3115	L	388	479	152	368	497	425	359	144	336	3148	6263		
										2992	A										3044	6036		
MIDDLE *Middle/Standard*	335	368	372	167	350	328	146	498	314	2878	Y	362	451	140	334	489	409	347	119	307	2958	5836		
										2775	E										2774	5549		
STANDARD *Standard/Forward*	320	331	348	127	307	274	119	456	301	2583	R	326	436	124	325	427	347	322	110	274	2691	5274		
										2423											2489	4912		
FORWARD	269	313	312	107	290	239	101	388	273	2292		293	395	95	260	367	308	273	81	212	2284	4576		
Burey												4	5	4	4	4	7	X	4	①				
Mallon												3	3	3	3	3	4	3	2					
PAR	4	4	4	3	4	4	3	5	4	35		4	5	3	4	5	4	4	3	4	36	71		
MEN'S HDCP	11	7	3	15					1	13		10	6	16	12	4	2	8	18	14				
LADIES' HDCP	7	5				11			1	13		12	4	16	10	6	2	8	18	14				
SCORER:											ATTEST:									DATE:				

RATING/SLOPE

MEN
Tournament 70.9/131
Back 69.6/128
Back/Middle 68.9/127
Middle 67.6/122
Middle/Standard 65.9/119
Standard 64.2/114
Standard/Forward 63.4/112
Forward 61.8/108

LADIES
Middle 73.5/132
Middle/Standard 71.4/127
Standard 70.0/125
Standard/Forward 68.4/117
Forward 66.4/114

JOHN'S ISLAND CLUB
South Course

Bill had talent but what was most impressive was his focus and the work ethic that he displayed working on his golf game. His intention was not only to make the PGA tour but also to be a dominant player. His regimen was extraordinary in that his program included strength training, flexibility workouts, endurance, and of course working on all aspects of his game. Bill's golf teacher and his coach was Bill Strausbaugh from Maryland, and I know Strausbaugh had never coached a golfer more dedicated. Mallon played smart and it was always fun to play with Bill and watch him manage his game.

One evening I asked Bill if he would play 9 holes. I think playing must have been on his schedule because he agreed. We played the John's Island South course back nine. He began by making birdie on the 10th and eagle on the short par five 11th hole, putting me two down! He made par on the par 3 12th and I made bogey. Now three up Bill birdied the13th and eagled hole 14. I'm five down after five. I didn't finish the 15th hole and he makes par, and then proceeds to birdie the par 4 16th. I'm seven down after seven, frustrated, although I was enjoying watching as he was now 7 under par for 7 holes. The sun was setting fast and it was cooling off quickly. Bill was not cooling off as he hits it stiff with a nine iron at the par 3 158 yard 17th. He is about to go 8 under for 8 holes and it's almost dark. I get to the tee, sun setting, and hit my eight iron in the hole for an ace. I said, "Bill you aren't winning this hole." Bill's reply to me "I'll pick up the balls. It's dark let's go in." I often wonder if he would have birdied the 346 yard 18th

I do know he wasn't very impressed with my ace!

Bill was awarded his tour card on his very first try. He competed on the PGA Tour from 1975 to 1979 and then returned to Duke to study medicine. He graduated with an M.D.in1984. Dr. Mallon had an outstanding career as an Orthopedic Surgeon specializing in the shoulder and currently resides in New Hampshire and South Carolina.

The John's Island "Match." Another Story!

Burey/and Mallon vs. Indiana University golfers Roberts and Jackson

Pete Dye and a Lesson in Golf Course Construction

In the winter of 1975, along with two or three other young apprentice golf professionals, I was asked by Pete Dye to have lunch. Pete had designed the South course at John's Island Club in Vero Beach and was in the process of building the second course. He was on-site to oversee the progress of the new North course.

Pete with his wife and partner Alice

Pete Dye's John's Island, south course

During lunch, we eagerly listened to Pete's insights regarding the John's Island project, his philosophy on golf course design and construction. I know he enjoyed sharing his thoughts with some very motivated young golf professionals. What I will never forget about that experience was what Pete Dye said: "The most important thing to understand in building a golf course is…Water *always* flows downhill!" Common sense. But isn't that life?

John's Island Club, Vero Beach Florida

Hole #17 North

My Best Trip to Florida!

Winters in the northeast can be brutal and when you are a golfer it can even be depressing! Making the trek to Florida to stay and play golf is an annual event for many. The fortunate get to spend most of the winter in Florida and others may plan a short golfing vacation.

I grew up in Connecticut and was obsessed with golf! I practiced and played whenever I could. My life was focused, to a fault, on golf. I caddied, worked on the grounds crew at our local Country Club, and loved to compete. Winters were very difficult for me, but I filled my time with basketball. I always felt high school basketball was a great compliment to golf and enabled me to be in good physical shape for "Spring" golf

My trips to Florida began when I was in the Navy! I was stationed in Norfolk Virginia on the USS Laffey. When in port in the winter of 1969 I had to use some leave (time off). Most normal sailors would take this time and go home, relax, and see family and friends! Not Jeff! I would drive south and go to Jacksonville Florida Naval Air Station. I could stay on-base in the transit barracks and practice and play the Air Station golf course from dawn to dark! I would be by myself but never have a problem finding a game! For a "Golf addict," this was always great because, there were minimal expenses, a good course, and usually great weather.

My next experiences in Florida came as apprentice golf professional! I had worked the summer seasons (73,74, &75) at Wee Burn CC in Darien. In the winters I would make the trip to Vero Beach where I worked at John's Island Club. I thought I had it all! What a great place! 2 Pete Dye designed golf courses, fantastic membership, tremendous staff, nearly perfect weather, and I could practice or play most every day.

How could any trip to Florida be better than my 4 or 5 experiences?

You have probably noticed my life was always centered around golf and probably a bit extreme.

My trip to Florida in mid-January of 1977 was quite different, I was now a PGA member and ready to hopefully have a "Head" golf professional position beginning in the Spring. My plan was not to work at John's Island, but rather spend January and February on Marco Island with my great friend Rick Werner.

Rick and another good friend Jim McLean were both working on the island, and I planned on doing my regular stuff, like practicing and honing my game. You might think meeting "The Squire" Gene Sarazen, Roger Maris, and spending time with Ken Venturi might have been the highlight of this January trip or any other!

No way!

As I drove interstate 95 down the east coast of Florida, I was focused on getting to Miami and across the state to Marco. I stopped for gas in Vero Beach and decided to call my friend David Liddle. David and I had worked together at John's Island the 3 previous winters. I found a phone booth and called! David answered and I told him I was passing through and just wanted to say hi!

David, a bit surprised, said: "Jeff, spend the night here and drive south tomorrow!" I said, "I'm on a schedule and need to get to Marco Island." David was insistent! He said "tonight is your annual cookout at Round Island beach." I had started this tradition 3 years prior. I said again: "I can't! I must keep going!" Finally, David said: "I want you to meet this nice girl!" David didn't tell me she was beautiful inside and out. I reluctantly said; "okay" and called Rick and said plans had changed and I will be on Marco Island tomorrow!

That evening I met Cathy Pritchard and at that moment I knew this was potentially life-changing! I was instantly smitten! I've been told there is no such thing as: "Love at first sight," I don't believe that to be true. The more I got to know Cathy that evening the more I was taken aback.

I did go on to southeast Florida the next day but had this beautiful Florida young lady on my mind!

I met the "Squire" and Maris! Practiced and played with Ken Venturi, Rick, and Jim. In the evening I would go to a nearby phone booth! For hours I would feed the phone quarters and talk with this Cathy Pritchard girl!

I never missed the PGA Merchandise Show and on January 27th, 1977 I asked Cathy to go to Orlando with me! Kind of like a first date! We had a great day and Cathy met many of my friends from the golf business, I had so much fun being with her.

At the Show I was offered the Head golf professional position at Pinehurst's new number Six course. I accepted and had to start February 1st, 4 days later

Before driving to Connecticut and back to Pinehurst I met Cathy's amazing mom and dad! We only met for a few minutes, but I knew they were special folks!

Pinehurst is just over 600 miles from Vero Beach which is not great for a relationship

Cathy continued to work at John's Island Club. I think we set records for our phone bills. We were able to visit and on occasion meet, but it was difficult as we were both busy with our jobs!

In May of 1978, Cathy left her position at John's Island and moved to Pinehurst. Cathy worked as a "sales manager" at the Pinehurst Hotel.

Village Chapel

Over the past 4 decades, I have played the very best courses in Florida. (Seminole, TPC Sawgrass "Stadium", Jupiter Hills, Black Diamond, Pine Tree, and dozens more! Great golf experiences!

Cathy and I were married on July 19th, 1978 in the Village Chapel in Pinehurst! We have been blessed with 4 wonderful kids and 9 precious grandkids.

This 40 plus year journey has been remarkable and we have been together every step of the way! I've been blessed for sure!

With all my trips to Florida, there will never be one that compares to that January 1977! My best trip ever, for sure!

Pinehurst
North Carolina

$100 to Hook It!

In November of 1976, I had completed all my PGA membership requirements and become a member of the Association. In late January of 1977, I was hired at the Pinehurst Resort and Country Club's new Fazio designed number 6 golf course and was to be the Head Golf Professional. Unlike the first five Pinehurst courses, which are operated out of one location, the number 6 course was developed 3 miles away. I had been in the golf business for only about three years, to be at Pinehurst was beyond belief and I was so excited to have the Head Professional position.

After arriving at Pinehurst, I was welcomed by a few surprises. I would say I hadn't done my homework. In retrospect, the surprises and opportunities hence made for one of the luckiest and most worthwhile opportunities imaginable and an incredible career in the golf business. First, the number 6 course was not even close to opening. Second, I'd be working at the main clubhouse. Third, I'd be working for Jay Overton, whom I had never met. Fourth, my main job would be to be a clerk in the main golf shop with two nice guys, both entry-level PGA apprentices. Fifth, beyond working the cash registers during the peak Spring season I could do whatever I thought would be beneficial to the Club. My passion, however, was teaching, and I couldn't foresee many lessons at this time.

I would describe the Spring season at Pinehurst as "crazy." On some days we would play more than 1500 golfers on five courses, all out of the one golf shop. Our day would begin, with the first tee times, shortly after dawn, and on most days, there would be numerous golf cars still out well after dark. We all knew that the Spring season was the time to "put the hay in the barn," and on many days I know we ran on sheer adrenalin.

On one Saturday afternoon, I was on station in the golf shop behind the counter. I think I was a little punchy as we were about to complete the busiest week of the season. I needed a break.

About that time a man in his early 50s entered the golf shop. I was concerned because he looked like he had been in a heavyweight boxing match. He was a mess, and I could tell very frustrated. He had this scary look of despair and had just come off the # 5 course where there is lots of Out of Bounds, especially to the right. He approached the counter and said, "I will pay anyone $100 who can make me hook it!" Without hesitating, I said, "I'm your man," jumped over the counter, and said, "Let's go." By the time we got to the range, he had cooled off, and my head had begun to clear. He relaxed and on his third swing hit the prettiest soft draw. I saw the relief on his face, and he reached into his pocket to pull a $100 bill. I said, "Please put it away. Hit a few more." After about 30 minutes we were both refreshed. I said "enjoy the next couple of days with us at Pinehurst" and refused to be paid. What he didn't know was I would have happily paid him the $100 to get out from behind that counter.

As things turned out I had an unbelievable experience at Pinehurst. My first Head Professional position, managing six golf courses at 28 years old.

Pinehurst #2

Pebble Beach "Bag Tags"

Pinehurst Resort was booming with golf in the spring of 1978. We had six golf courses, operating at full capacity and had assembled a great team to run the operation. As the head golf professional and a part of this well-oiled machine, it was a privilege for me.

Our days were long and as summer approached, we all needed a break to re-charge. The activity in June was relatively light, but from July to Thanksgiving it would be very busy. In early July, we hosted our national junior School of Golf, followed by the PGA Tour Hall of Fame Classic, Golf Digest schools, and dozens of corporate and charity events.

Lou Miller was my boss and had hired me twice. Lou is probably the most engaging individual I have ever met. Miller was vice president of Pinehurst and oversaw all the amenities at the resort and country club. Lou had an awesome job and I always felt that he had total confidence in me. I have never met or worked with anyone I respect more than Lou Miller. I would go to war with Lou, and he has been a friend and significant part of my life for four decades.

Sometime in early June of 78, Lou summoned me for a meeting. He said we (the two of us) would be making an important

Lou Miller

business trip to California. We would leave Sunday, June 11th, and return Friday, June 16th. When I asked the question: "where and why we were going? He said, "Pebble Beach, we need to see why they sell more golf bag tags than we do." Confused, I soon learned Lou had carefully planned much more.

On Sunday afternoon June 11th we flew from Greensboro to Denver and drove down to Colorado Springs. The Broadmoor had recently opened their new "Arnold Palmer" course, and Lou wanted to see how they handled their shuttle/ transportation from the hotel to the new course and back. Located some distance from their other two courses, this was like Pinehurst's situation with the Hotel and Pinehurst #6. We had a nice visit with Dow Finsterwald, who was very helpful, cordial, and a real gentleman.

Pebble Beach hole #18

On Tuesday morning we drove back to Denver and went to Cherry Hills to watch the practice round for the US Open. Besides seeing a great historic golf course, the purpose was to encourage players to come to Pinehurst for the Hall of Fame Classic in August. We had all access to Cherry Hills because we hosted a PGA tour stop. Lou knew so many players. I was in awe.

Tuesday evening, we flew again. Our destination this time was San Francisco.

On Wednesday morning, Lou had arranged for us to play the Lake course at Olympic Club. The 1966 US Open, won in a playoff by Billy Casper over Arnold Palmer, was etched in my mind. I remember we teed off in a dense fog and our caddies guided us for the first three holes. On the par-five 16th hole I birdied, and Lou reminded me of Casper's birdie and Palmer's bogey in 1966. Palmer had lost a seven-shot lead in the last nine holes.

Wednesday afternoon we drove down the California coast and, although we didn't play, we got to walk and see Dr. Mackenzie's Cypress Point.

The first tee time at Pebble Beach belonged to us on Thursday. I'll never forget that morning. We played in just over 3 hours. What a spectacular experience and place.

Back to San Francisco and home to Pinehurst Friday. Lou Miller had planned it all, and we were ready and rested for the remainder of 1978 at Pinehurst.

One of the many things I learned from Lou Miller was the importance of making memories, and I made many on that trip in 1978.

By the way, we still do not know why Pebble sold more Bag tags than we did.

The Good Doctor from Chapel Hill

I have always had tremendous respect for teachers! The best teachers have enthusiasm for their subject, can engage, motivate, and instill a love of learning in their students.

In the mid-seventies, I met a man who was a great teacher, impacted my life, and became a great friend.

Dr. Richard "Dick" Coop was Professor of Educational Psychology at the University of North Carolina at Chapel Hill. Dick was born and raised in Kentucky, graduated from Indiana University, was a professor at UNC. With his background, one might assume this is a basketball story.

However, Dick Coop loved all sports and was a consultant to all the athletic teams at UNC. His work with the golf team was particularly interesting to me.

In 1978 Dr. Coop co-authored a book with Dr. Gary Wiren, "The New Golf Mind." Their book was a great resource that most PGA teaching professionals found extremely helpful.

Dr. Coop, like most everyone, loved Pinehurst, loved to golf, and would often make the trip down from Chapel Hill. I think Lou Miller, Director of Golf and Vice President of Pinehurst introduced me to Dr. Coop, and instantly I liked this guy.

As Head Golf Professional and Director of Instruction, I was tasked with developing an adult golf school for the Resort guests. Pinehurst professionals Jim Sargent, Rod Loesch, and I built the model and the "Pinehurst Golf Advantage" schools became a reality. We would have 20-24 students with wide ranges of experience and often couples from all over the country! The feedback from these schools was very positive. The final day of the golf school would end with a dinner at the Pinehurst hotel. The dinners were great, but the highlight was always the presentation by Dr. Richard Coop. He added the "WOW" factor for the final evening.

When we moved on to Wolf Creek in Olathe Kansas in 1981. Dick Coop would make the trip to Kansas just for me. His presentation for a member's night drew a full house and my membership had their expectations exceeded.

Dr. Coop spoke to many PGA Sections and came to our Midwest Section in 1982. His presentation is still one of the Sections' best!

Dick and his wife Sharon made one more trip to Kansas in 2010. His presentation for the Prairie Dunes membership and guests was better than ever. What a professional and friend!

In 1993 Dr. Coop published his second book titled "Mind Over Golf" and he and Dr. Robert Rotella co-authored an audiotape/workbook which has been used by teaching professionals, low handicap amateurs, and tour professionals.

Over the years Dick Coop has consulted with professional and amateur athletes from most sports (Baseball, basketball, football, and even NASCAR drivers) as well as coaches, primarily Football and Basketball.

Dr. Coop has worked with dozens of professional golfers as well, including Payne Stewart, Corey Pavin, Ben Crenshaw, Larry Mize, Nick Faldo, Scott Simpson, Mark O'Meara, and many more have spent time with Dr. Dick.

Dr. Coop has impacted many lives but no one more than my wife Cathy and me. Dick counseled and guided us through the most difficult and tragic time of our life when our seven month old son Matthew died. We are forever grateful to him for his tender counsel to us.

I will always treasure my relationship with The Good Doctor from Chapel Hill.

Dr. Richard Coop

Pinehurst "Golf a Thon"

Pinehurst Resort and Country Club is considered by many to be the Golf Capital of the World. Golfers from all over the world will make the trip to the Sandhills of North Carolina to test their skills and experience unbelievable golf. Springtime, March 1st to May 30th, is the peak season. Tee times are booked solid from dawn to a couple of hours before dark and with six courses (in 1978) it makes for long days! Yet the excitement of all the activity made it easier to stay enthusiastic and those long days seemed shorter!

On Friday mornings Lou Miller, Pinehurst Director of Golf would schedule 5:00 AM (1 hour) staff meetings. There were about 10 of us who would be invited. These meetings were very useful in many ways. Yes, 5:00 AM! Although challenging to get there on time, a review of events and a look ahead was worthwhile. The last item on the agenda was always Lou's question, "What ideas would you like to share?"

I had many ideas and occasionally, had a good one! At one of the March meetings, I presented what turned out to be a big idea. I proposed that another guy and I play all six Pinehurst courses in one day! The plan was outlined with the Five W's and H. The Who, What, Where, When, Why, and How were all addressed!

The idea was well-received, approved, and an event to be called the Pinehurst Golf a Thon was going to happen.

Michael Dann

This group could make things happen and boy did they!

Michael Dann, Golf World Magazine reporter/ writer, good player, and friend would be the other player. Michael was a fun guy, with a sharp wit, creative, and competitive. He lived in Pinehurst and with the magazine based in Southern Pines, Michael had great connections not only locally but also with the national golf community.

We planned to play the 108 holes in one day. The event would benefit the PGA of America's, National Golf Day Charities. We would have a contest to see who could come closest to guessing our total score for the twelve rounds. We had a tie-breaker, by guessing our total birdies and eagles. There was no entry fee, but people were encouraged to contribute. Local sponsors were asked to step up!

We would play all the six courses beginning with the brand new Tom Fazio Number Six course and finish by walking the famous Donald Ross Number Two. I mentioned Michael was competitive. Michael was determined and let everyone know he was going to best the Big pro.

We had to consider daylight because we didn't know how much time we would need or potential weather challenges. July 9th was chosen because it was close to the longest day of the year and we needed all the daylight possible.

The "Why" part of this story is important. I had read an article about a fellow PGA golf professional, Randy Smith, at Royal Oaks, in Dallas. I didn't know Randy but learned that he had led the nation in National Golf Day fundraising for at least a dozen years in a row. Michael and I decided that streak would end. Michael had the PR resources and we had the support of Pinehurst and its great people.

The date set, contest with rules decided, police escort from Number Six course, official scorers invited, forecaddies assigned and a plan for how to manage the event with the regular daily play on all six courses was set.

We were ready!

Michael Dann stepped up and multiple press releases were sent out. The pre-event publicity was unbelievable. Newspapers in Raleigh, Greensboro, Fayetteville, and even Atlanta had before and after stories. The Golf a Thon was featured in Golf Digest, Golf Magazine, Golf World, Sports Illustrated (Scorecard), and was even featured on a Paul Harvey radio segment. Michael had done his job!

Most of the Radio stations in the mid-south conducted interviews and their questions were usually similar. Are you both physically prepared? Do you have the stamina? Do you have enough daylight? Could this possibly be a Guinness record? Michael's favorite question was: "Which one of you will shoot the lower score." Without hesitation, Dann would say always "Me!"

On July 9, 1978

Michael and I did it!

Six Courses were played before dark! The weather was perfect!

Total golfing time was 11 hours and 57 minutes!

Pinehurst led the Nation for "National Golf Day" contributions, with Randy Smith finishing second!

Overall contest winner received a (4 Day 3 Night) golf package, for four, at the Pinehurst Hotel!

Our total score was 924

We made a total of 19 birdies and eagles!

The day wasn't perfect, Michael Dann edged me out with a 6 round total score of 459 to mine of 465!

Memories from that day are so special and the entire Pinehurst team executed the event with precision!

Is playing six different regulation golf courses in one day a Guinness record? I'm still not sure!

Stories in the Life of a Golf Professional!

the official publication of the
Professional Golfers' Association of America

OCTOBER 1978

MAGAZINE

GOLF-A-THON
TEAMWORK
TOPS NATIONAL
GOLF DAY

Tour School, the All American, and a Night in Jail!

The PGA "Tour Qualifying School" has evolved over the years! Today the top 25 money winners on the Korn Ferry tour earn their cards and PGA Tour status. Also, the Korn Ferry finals determine the remaining 25, card earners!

The "Q" school format often changed, but usually resembled a marathon! It was common for this career-launching event to be 144 holes. Some years there would be one qualifier and other years two (Spring and Fall). In 1977 Regional qualifiers were held and the Fall PGA "Q" school final was reduced to 72 holes with a 36-hole cut.

Jim McLean started his professional career in 1973. We met and became friends in 1975. Jim and another great friend, Rick Werner, and I taught golf all day, 6 days a week! Jim at Westchester CC in Harrison NY, Rick at Quaker Ridge in Scarsdale NY, and me at Wee Burn in Darien Connecticut. On Mondays, we would sometimes play! I would love it when we would share ideas about our teaching! Good stuff!

In January of 1977, while visiting Werner on Marco Island (Jim McLean was also there for the winter), I was introduced to Ken Venturi by Jim. Venturi was working with Jim in preparation for McLean's future on tour! The four of us would practice together almost every afternoon and some days play a few holes. The chemistry between Venturi and McLean was amazing. Being a student of the game, the opportunity for Jim to work with Ken Venturi was priceless.

Jim's playing resume was already impressive! As an amateur McLean won the Washington State Junior Championship, qualified for the USGA Junior Am, won numerous Pacific coast tournaments, and 3 times qualified for the USGA Amateur. Jim had qualified and played in the 1971 and 1972 US Opens'! In 1972 he was invited and competed in the "Masters." He made the cut and finished 43rd. From

1969-1973 McLean was at the University of Houston and was an All -American. Jim could golf!

The 1977 "Fall" Tour Qualifying school was at Pinehurst and I was finishing my first season on staff at the resort and country club. I got a phone call from Jim McLean and he said he was coming to Pinehurst for the Tour school final. I said: "Fantastic", plan on staying with me! I have a 2-bedroom apartment and I'm 2 minutes from the main clubhouse!"

Jim McLean

Jim arrived and was in a great frame of mind! He had breezed through the regional qualifier and seemed comfortable and happy with his game. The kid from Westchester had 3 days to practice, prepare and map out the Pinehurst number 4 course. Jim's practice rounds were consistently under par, and all areas of his game seemed finely tuned. He was very disciplined, eating well, getting plenty of sleep, and confident.

Jim McLean was ready!

The afternoon before the start of the "Qualifying" school, Jim had a plan. A relaxing evening, good dinner, to bed early and he would be set for the warm-up and 8:00 am tee time for the first round.

At about 4:30 I was in the Golf shop and Jim had finished his practice and stopped in. He said he was going to Southern Pines (5 miles away) to pick up some things and head back to the apartment. I said:" I would be home at 6:00 or so."

At about 5:45 the phone in the shop rings and is answered by, Brenda, one of our staff. I remember being with a member when Brenda says: "Jim McLean is on the phone and needs you!" I said: "please just tell him I will be there in about 20 minutes!" Brenda

Jim McLean

then says" "Jeff, he says they are putting him in jail!" I said: "He's a practical joker, just tell him I will be home shortly." As I'm leaving to go home Brenda says: "I don't think he was kidding!" I decide to call the Southern Pines police station and ask the deputy if there is a blond guy named Jim McLean there. The deputy says: "We are locking that son of a ...... up right now."

My thoughts: What the heck is going on? This is crazy!

I drive to Southern Pines to try to figure things out!

Turns out Jim McLean, in his brand new, silver, Dodge Charger, with red pinstripes, and New York tags had made his way to the town of Southern Pines. He picked up his dry cleaning and at the grocery store, bought eggs, milk, and a couple of steaks to grill for dinner.

As Jim exits the grocery store, he is approached by the deputy sheriff who asks: "Is that your car?" McLean says: "Yes!" The sheriff says: "Do you know what you just did?" Jim says: "Bought some eggs, milk, and steaks" Wrong answer! The sheriff says: "you wise ......! You went thru a 30 miles per hour zone at almost 60!" Our future Tour pro makes another double bogey and says: "I have a radar detector and it didn't go off! How do you know I was speeding?" The deputy has had enough! Groceries and dry-cleaning inside the car were locked, Jim McLean handcuffed, driven to the police station in the patrol car, and booked. Jim's one phone call hadn't helped his situation a bit.

When I arrived at the police station and heard the story, I couldn't believe it! What had been a perfect start to the week was now a nightmare.

I contacted an attorney and Jim was released on bail with a $300.00 bond in the wee hours of the night! We retrieved his car and arrived at the apartment shortly before dawn.

With a trial date to be set, no dinner, hardly any sleep, McLean tees off at 8:00 AM. The first-round score of 77 is recorded.

The next morning it's back to the Southern Pines jail with the lawyer to complete some paperwork. After reliving the events of the past day and a half Jim shoots 73 in the afternoon second round. His 150 total misses the 36-hole cut by 1.

That Tour qualifying school changed the career path for an amazing golf professional and friend!

Jim McLean is a world-renowned golf instructor, author, businessman, and contributor to the Game. Jim has impacted thousands of golfers and dozens of the elite, men, and women tour professionals.

What's your guess? What might the career of Jim McLean look like today, if he hadn't met that Southern Pines sheriff deputy in 1977?

Go West Young Man!

The Delta flight from Raleigh, thru Atlanta lands at Kansas City International airport (KCI)! It's late Saturday afternoon January 3rd of 1981. The University of North Carolina Chapel Hill is in town to play basketball against the Kansas University Jayhawks. The battle of these "bluebloods" is in Kemper Arena.

I'm not here for the game, but for an opportunity that would change my career and life!

I was going to Olathe Kansas to interview for the position of Head Golf Professional and General Manager at Wolf Creek Golf Club.

My interview was scheduled for the next morning (Sunday) at 9:00 am.

I checked in, at the Best Western hotel at the first Olathe exit on Interstate 35. I asked the desk clerk how far I was from Wolf Creek Golf Club and he said he had no idea, never heard of the place. I went to a nearby gas station to get directions and again the attendant couldn't help. Back at the hotel, a little nervous, I called the President of the club and he gave me the directions. Willis Ashley was also the chairman of the selection committee. Feeling a bit more comfortable, I watched the KU-UNC game and pondered what might be in store for tomorrow.

Sunday morning, I was up at 6:00 and ready to go at 7:00! The morning temperature was 5 degrees! I walked to the Denny's next to the hotel and had breakfast.

I arrived at Wolf Creek for the first time at 8:15 and as I entered thru the double doors of the clubhouse, I was greeted by three golfers. The temperature was still single digits, wind howling out of the north, and the ground frozen, hard as a rock! The three were heading to the 1st tee, dressed in layers of fleece, long handles, and wearing ski masks with only their eyes showing. I thought: "These guys are crazy! Where am I?"

I entered the Golf shop and met Brad Sater. Brad was a golf professional on staff.

One of the members of the selection committee came in, introduced himself, and said my interview would be delayed. The committee was going to interview another candidate ahead of me because one of the members was going to be late and they wanted him there for my meeting.

Brad Sater showed me thru the clubhouse and answered quite a few of my questions. He went to the basement, drove up a golf cart, and was going to show me some of the golf course. It was so cold the course tour didn't last very long.

On the way in, I asked to stop at the nearby 9th green. We walked over and I looked down and in the dead of winter saw a putting surface that was perfect. I had grown up in Connecticut and knew what winter dormant greens usually looked like! This green had no blemishes, was as smooth as glass, and had nothing but beautiful bent grass.

We returned to the clubhouse, I thanked Brad, and it was time for my interview!

Wolf Creek hole #1

I met Willis Ashley for the first time, and he led the way to the Board room. I was introduced to the 8 or 9 other members of the committee and we all took our seats, Ashley at one end of the table and me at the other.

I had researched and learned a little about Wolf Creek and was excited but comfortable. Ashley was the point person for the committee, and he related a short history of the club and its philosophy. I will always remember these words: "Jeff we are all busy folks and are at Wolf Creek to relax! We want to hire someone who will manage this club and lead. We do not want to be at all involved with the day to day operation. We will be available if needed but otherwise, we just want to play golf!"

The interview was fantastic! They had excellent questions and I felt my answers were direct and concise. I later learned the other candidate's interviews had lasted an hour and mine was 3 hours! I felt, because of my questions, I learned much more about the club and was very impressed.

At the end of the meeting, Mr. Ashley thanked me and said they would be contacting me.

I drove back to KCI and made my evening flight back to North Carolina! I got home to Southern Pines and recapped the trip and experience with Cathy, my wife. Now it's time to wait!

Monday morning at about 8:00, Cathy and I are having breakfast and again discussing the Kansas possibilities and the future. The phone rings and it's Willis Ashley. He says, "Good morning!" and gets right to the point. "We would like to offer you the job!" I hadn't expected to hear from them in less than 24 hours and was a little shocked. I said, "thank you", but said Cathy has never been to Kansas City and I would like to take her to get a feel for Johnson County Kansas. Ashley said: "No problem. Book your flight and we will take care of the rest!"

I was all in and ready for a new opportunity. The question was: Would Cathy agree and leave the beautiful sandhills of North Carolina and move to a place, not knowing a soul, and start a new journey?

Cathy and I flew to Kansas City on Friday and the club had a car waiting. Our hotel was the Alameda on the Country Club Plaza and this was not the Best Western. We spent Saturday meeting many people and Cathy toured Johnson county with Nancy Kirk (wife of Frank, who was a founding Wolf Creek member and on the selection committee) The Ashley's and the Kirk's took us to a very nice restaurant "Jaspers" and we had a wonderful dinner and evening on Saturday night! We were treated like Royalty!

We still had a gigantic decision to make!

On Sunday we returned to North Carolina and on Monday I, with Cathy's support, officially accepted the position at Wolf Creek.

On February 2nd 1981 we arrived in Kansas and on February 3rd I began my 27-year tenure at the "Creek."

The Wolf Creek experience was a perfect match for the club and a young guy from the East. For over 4 decades Kansas has been an unbelievable home for the Bureys!

By the way, Kansas beat North Carolina that cold Saturday night at Kansas Cities Kemper Arena. The score was 56-55 in a classic battle of the Big's.

Horace Greeley was right!

Wolf Creek hole #11

Wolf Creek

Prairie Dunes Kansas & Beyond

The US Open and the Golf Bag

The 1999 US Open at Pinehurst Resort was played on the famous Donald Ross Number 2 course and will always be remembered as the Payne Stewart Championship. A spectacular finish with Stewart besting Phil Mickelson by one shot. This Open will always have personal significance for me as it demonstrates the thoughtfulness and kindness of a great champion.

First a little backdrop!

My wife Cathy and I moved to Kansas from Pinehurst in February of 1981. I had been hired by the Wolf Creek Golf Club to be their Golf Director/ General Manager. Although just 11 years old Wolf Creek had a reputation as a pure golf club. The Creek had a great layout, was a home club for the best players in the greater Kansas City area, and maybe the best greens in all the Midwest. Wolf Creek was always fun to play and a very special place.

In 1979 the Creek hosted the Missouri Amateur Championship and the winner was a confident, talented, young blond kid from Springfield, Missouri Payne Stewart. Payne defeated the Walker Cup team member and outstanding amateur Jim Holtgrieve in the 36-hole final.

During my tenure on staff and as the head golf professional at Pinehurst (1977-1981) we hosted four "Hall of Fame Classic" tour events. The winners were Hale Irwin in 1977, Tom Watson in 1978 and 1979, and Phil Hancock in 1980. I had met Tom Watson because I had helped coordinate a clinic which Tom led for all the area, junior golfers. He did this each year before the Hall of Fame.

Tom was professional, gracious, genuine, and a great ambassador for the game. The kids and all of us loved it!

Back to the story!

June of 1999, just before the 99th US Open Tom Watson comes into my Wolf Creek golf shop and asks "Jeff, do you have a nice large golf bag I might buy and take to the Open?" I showed him the nicest bag in the shop, a leather Steerhide, Burton, classic, with the Wolf Creek Logo embroidered on the ball pocket. The bag had a hefty price tag, but Tom didn't flinch. He said, "I'll take it, put it on my account!" I said "Thanks" and out the door, he went! I later figured out he was probably between contracts with longtime sponsor Ram and future sponsor Adams and needed a golf bag.

Watson could have gotten a golf bag from any of 100 places but chose Wolf Creek and me! He took that bag to Pinehurst without his name on it, only the Wolf Creek logo.

The week of the Open at least 50 phone calls (friends, fellow golf professionals, former neighbors, and Pinehurst members) from the Sandhills of North Carolina came to my office in Kansas. I couldn't

believe how many folks had seen Tom Watson with his Wolf Creek golf bag on Pinehurst Number 2

Tom Watson didn't have his best Open in 1999 at Pinehurst. He made the cut and played 72 holes. Tom again showed me his kindness and heart. He did it for me!

Payne Stewart won the 1999 United States Open and Tom Watson won me!

In 2018 Tom gave me the bag back!

Advice Twice

Most PGA sections have a few, or at least, one outstanding player. These folks seem to dominate in their local tournaments

The Midwest PGA Section has Robert J Wilkin, AKA Rob/Robbie/Wilk. Born March 29th 1961 in Ottumwa, Iowa, Rob has lived most of his life in the Sunflower State and we claim him as a Kansan!

Rob attended, played golf, and graduated from Coffeyville, Kansas Community College in 1981. Wilk graduated from Kansas University in 1983. Wilkin played for Ross Randall, Jayhawk golf coach, and was team captain his senior year. Rob has played in 10 major championships, won 16 Section Championships, and been Section "Player of the Year" 18 times. Rob is our player!

I was always fortunate to have fantastic apprentice professionals at my club of 27 years. Wolf Creek Golf Club always had excellent players on our staff.

In January of 1984, I received a letter and phone call from Randall. He said Rob Wilkin had decided he would like to pursue a career in the Golf business. Ross thought Wolf Creek, Rob, and I would be a good fit. Rob and I scheduled a meeting/interview and Ross was right. I knew Rob was very talented, competitive, and confident. What I learned later was how disciplined, humble, polite, quietly engaging, and what a great leader he was.

Rob Wilkin came on staff in March of 1984 and almost immediately bonded with the membership. (Even the Missouri University guys) Rob's personality and talent for golf made for a perfect fit!

Wilkin and I even had some team golf success. One year he and I won the Section Pro-Assistant championship. Rob shot 67. I helped one shot and with our score of 66 we were in a playoff with three other teams. Of course, Rob birdied the first hole of the playoff for our win.

In 1998 Rob advanced thru the US Open local qualifier in Kansas City. He moved on to the Sectionals in St. Louis at Bellerive Country Club. After shooting 72 in the morning, he shot 68 in the afternoon. Rob Wilkin had qualified for his first US Open. The 1988 Open would be contested, at The Country Club, in Brookline Massachusetts. The Wolf Creek membership and Kansas City golf community were excited to have a second golf professional from Kansas in the "1988 Open" field.

Before leaving for Boston, Rob asked to talk with me. I think I was as happy and excited as he was that he had qualified! Rob knew I had played in three Hall of Fame classics (host Professional exemption) at Pinehurst. He asked if I had any advice. Good question! The standard, the simple answer was: "Try to relax, have fun, enjoy the experience, be yourself, and trust that you are prepared and ready." Coach talk!

As I pondered Rob's question, my mind flashed back to my Pinehurst experience. Thoughts that entered my head were gigantic galleries, staying focused, adrenalin spiking, and maybe some fear. With those negative vibes from 10 or so years earlier, I had an answer. My Advice: "If possible, play your practice rounds with the most high-profile players, and try to preview and anticipate what might be in store for the Thursday start."

Rob Wilkin arrived in Boston Sunday evening and went to the golf course on Monday morning. Lockers are assigned to the competitors alphabetically. Wilkin's locker was next to another Kansas competitor Watson. Rob wrote a note and taped it to Watson's locker. Our man Rob asked Tom if they might play a practice round together.

That Monday afternoon Rob was on the practice tee, practicing, next to one of his heroes Lee Trevino. Tom Watson approaches Rob. Says he is playing at 9:00 am the next day and invites Rob to play. Trevino hears the invite and asks, "Do you have room for me?" Yes, they did!

Tuesday arrives and the 9:00 tee time looms! Wilkin and his caddy are in rush hour traffic and the clock is ticking. They arrive at the "Player" parking lot at 8:50. Rob throws his shoes on, grabs his clubs, racing to the first tee as his caddy parks the car. Arriving at the tee at exactly 9:00, shoes untied, no warm-up, with Watson and Trevino waiting. The gallery is huge and excited to see the two former US Open Champions.

Tom and Lee hit nice solid drives that fly straight down the middle. Rob steps up, shoes still untied, right out of the car, and launches a drive that carries 300 yards to a white painted line used to measure the Long Drive.

Rod is last to hit his second shot and knocks it stiff for a Kick away birdie. Walking to the second tee, Lee Trevino says to Rob "Kid, don't peak too early."

Rob went on to make the cut in the 1988 US Open and finish with a score of 295 (74,71,77, & 73).

Rob Wilkin is currently Golf Director and manages the Heritage Park Golf Course for the Johnson County Parks and Recreation Department. Wilkin has served in leadership positions for the Midwest PGA Section for many years and continues to play outstanding golf. Rob is a giant in our Midwest PGA Section and I'm certain Rob Wilkin has offered great advice to hundreds!

Rob Wilkin with Brian Coens

Fletcher

Next year that ball will be right there!

Fletcher Gaines was one of many exceptional caddies at Pinehurst Resort and Country Club. He was also very special to me and was a true Gentleman, soft-spoken, polite, incredibly professional, small in stature but gigantic in character, a true ambassador for Pinehurst and golf. He was a third-generation caddie, he had a  great relationship with Curtis Strange and hundreds of other golfers of all skill levels. Fletcher Gaines was the caddie of choice for all major events held on Donald Ross's Pinehurst Number 2. He could bring out the very best in players and his golfers would almost always exceed their abilities and expectations.

On one of many trips back to Pinehurst from Kansas, I coordinated a visit for eleven members of my club. None of the players had ever been to Pinehurst, although most had traveled on numerous golf vacations. There was great enthusiasm and anticipation for this trip. I had put together a full itinerary for the boys. We would stay at the historic Pinecrest Inn; have fabulous breakfasts and Family style dinners. We would visit the World Golf Hall of Fame, the Tuft's archive and experience the charm of the village. I had set up five rounds of golf at the finest courses in the sandhills of North Carolina. I take joy from making memories, and this trip would produce many.

This group of members, although middle to high handicappers, loved golf and the fellowship (gambling) that goes with the game. Victor Fontana, a Kansas City restauranteur, and great guy carried a handicap in the mid-20s and was rarely on the winning side of his matches. Everybody loves Vic but Victor's luck had not changed the first two days of our trip. He lost every bet! I knew he was determined to get even with the final round on the championship Number 2 course. I set the pairings for the final round and paired Vic in the final foursome with me. At dinner, the night before the conversation was about how much fun the trip was and how exciting it would be to play, with caddies, Donald Ross' premier golf course. I knew this would be the climax of an unbelievable trip and knew memories would last lifetimes. The first two groups teed off and before hitting the tee I introduced our caddies to my members. When I introduced Fletcher to Victor, I noticed a twinkle in the professional caddie's eye. On the very first green, putting for par 4 Victor left his putt hanging on the lip of the hole. As Victor stalled hoping the putt might drop, the quiet and reserved Fletcher said "Mr. Fontana, that ball will be right there when you come back next year." I noticed instant chemistry between the two and when the round was over Victor had won most if not all his losses back. I'm certain Fletcher was the big winner for the day. Fletcher had a wonderful gift of understanding people. In my book, he is among the great. There were some great memories from this trip, and I couldn't help but think how much fun Fletcher Gaines provided and how many thousands of lives he has impacted.

May God bless Fletcher Gaines!

Pinecrest Inn, Village of Pinehurst, North Carolina

A Guy Named Bill!
"Part Two"

I had met Bill in 1973 while on the winter professional staff at John's Island Club in Vero Beach Florida. It has been a privilege to closely follow Bill Coore's career since the beginning, know this talented great guy, and for him to be a friend.

In 1985, while Golf Director/ General Manager at Wolf Creek Golf Club in Olathe Kansas, I met a developer from Lincoln Nebraska, Dick Youngscap. Dick knew lots of folks from Kansas City and was working on a golf course project in Lincoln. His goal was to build a great Golf club and course. Dick liked the simplicity and I would say had an appreciation for our minimalist philosophy at the Creek. I can't remember who introduced us, but I met with Dick for most of a day. He wanted to learn about some of the things Wolf Creek did well and how he might incorporate those things at his new club. I think he went home with a few good ideas.

Lot's more here, but the bottom line is Dick hired the renowned golf course architect Pete Dye and they built a fabulous course. Firethorn Golf Club is the only Pete Dye course in Nebraska and one of Dye's very best anywhere!

In the early '90s, probably 1992 I receive a phone call and it's Bill Coore. He starts with a question: "Jeff, where do you think I am?" I said "Hawaii, Arizona, Long Island, Texas." He said: "No, No, No! Ben and I are here at the airport in North Platte Nebraska." (Google North Platte Canteen for an amazing American Story). Startled I said: "What for?" He said something like: We may attempt one of the craziest things ever. We just saw the perfect piece of ground to build a golf course and think we are going to do it! The team of Bill Coore and Ben Crenshaw returned to Austin.

I pondered what I had just heard. Imagine a golf course 60 miles northeast of North Platte in Mullen, Nebraska. The property is in Hooker county with a population of 600 and a golf season that would be a maximum of four months. Crazy! The obstacles seemed overwhelming to me.

Turns out Dick Youngscap, the visionary from Lincoln, had surveyed several thousand acres and with Coore and Crenshaw identified over 100 possible holes. I think Bill and Ben would say they discovered the holes, that already had been naturally placed there.

The next call I received, a while later, was from Dick Youngscap. He said 18 holes had been routed and he suggested I charter a plane, handpick a group of seven or so, Kansas City, folks, and come see the site. He gave me a date when both Bill and Ben would be there. Done! I contacted a Wolf Creek member with a plane (King Air) and he flew seven of us to North Platte. At the airport, we split into two foursomes. Four would fly to the site by helicopter and the other four would make the drive.

At the site, we were greeted by the threesome (Dick, Bill, and Ben). We had a guided tour, walked most of the 18 holes that had been plotted. Listening to Bill and Ben's thoughts and ideas was something special. I clearly remember standing in the middle of

what was to be and is now the second fairway. Ben described the short par four, with two greens in one (high on the right, low on the left) with a false front. Crenshaw explained how precise the short iron approach shot had to be to have a birdie putt or even stay on the green.

In every way, our group had what today you might call a Bucket List experience.

I later remember a phone conversation as to what this place might be named. I think Bill Coore chose the appropriate descriptive name Sand Hills. My thought was there might be confusion because of the Sandhills of North Carolina. Bill said I'm confident "Sand Hills" in Mullen Nebraska will stand on its own.

Coming back from a summer family trip to Vail, Colorado, we decided to take the Interstate 80 northern route and detour to see the Sand Hills Golf Club progress. The course was now growing-in. Dick was building the clubhouse and I think had

one lodge already built. It was another great afternoon as we toured, with Dick guiding us around this "Masterpiece."

Sand Hills maybe my favorite place to visit and has been a gift to me for over 25 years. I believe a trip to Sand Hills Golf Club is as great a golf experience as any. I don't know the number of people from all over the country (the people at SHGC know that number) that I have hosted, but I certainly know how proud I am to have been a small part of the Sand Hills story. Bill Coore was right Sand Hills, in Mullen Nebraska, has a reputation all its own

Thank you, Dick, Ben, and Bill!

I am so glad "I met a guy named Bill"

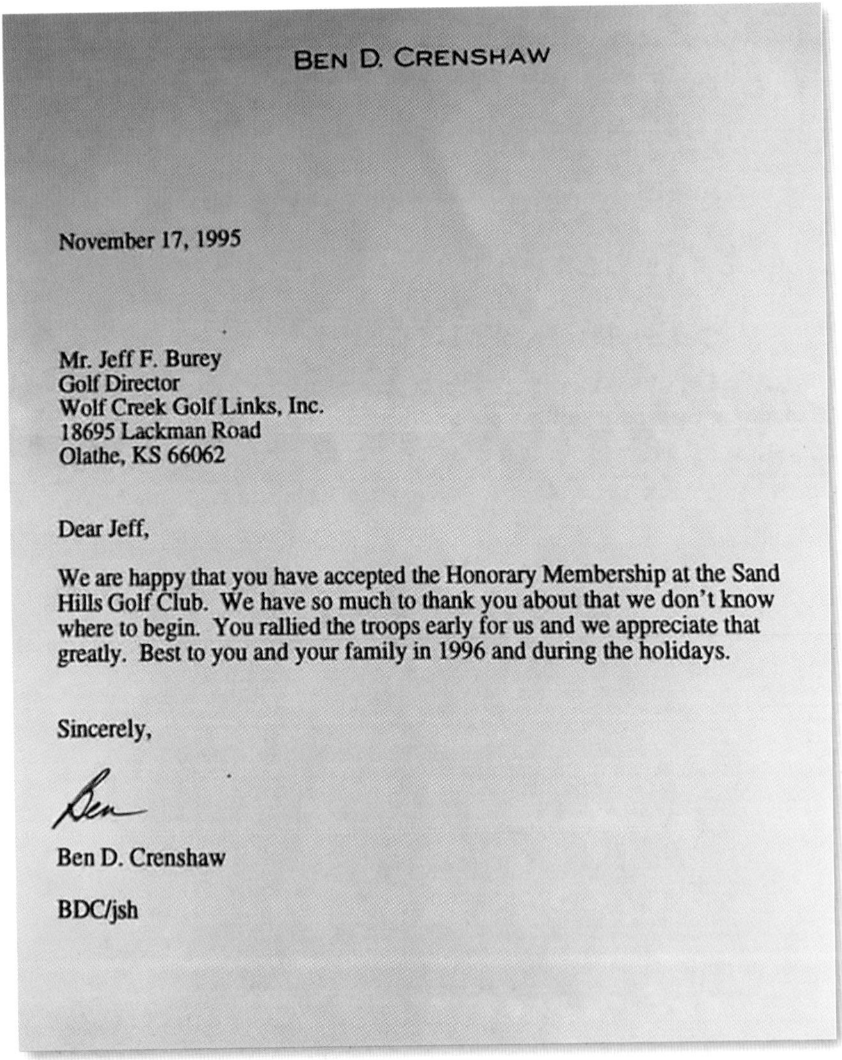

BEN D. CRENSHAW

November 17, 1995

Mr. Jeff F. Burey
Golf Director
Wolf Creek Golf Links, Inc.
18695 Lackman Road
Olathe, KS 66062

Dear Jeff,

We are happy that you have accepted the Honorary Membership at the Sand Hills Golf Club. We have so much to thank you about that we don't know where to begin. You rallied the troops early for us and we appreciate that greatly. Best to you and your family in 1996 and during the holidays.

Sincerely,

Ben

Ben D. Crenshaw

BDC/jsh

Boom-Boom Changed John's Mind!

With an effortless swing, he launches the four wood! Like a laser, the ball takes off on the perfect trajectory and lands softly on the green. The 287-yard shot bounces once and rolls 6 feet and comes to rest 30 inches from the hole. That's a kick-away eagle on the par 5.

It's 1992 at Wolf Creek Golf Club in Olathe Kansas and I'm beginning my second decade at the Creek. As Golf Professional, I had witnessed some amazing golf. Wolf Creek had an elite group of guys! The handicap, posted on the board, was the most important measure of their status.

Kansas City baseball legend George Brett was a member and always enjoyed playing golf with the club's best players! In 1992 George was still focused on swinging the baseball bat but the challenge of golf had become another passion. Being a great athlete and driven to excel, we all watched as his game quickly improved.

Brett, Brian Irvine, Dan Wastler, JB, and Couples

George would spend some of the offseason at Mission Hills in the California desert and became friends with Fred Couples. George would play lots of golf and often with Fred.

In April of 1992, Fred Couples won the Masters, and that August Fred came to Kansas City to visit George Brett. George was a great host and they played some golf at Wolf Creek. Couples also got to do a few other things that Brett had planned, like pitching batting practice before a Kansas City Royals game at Kaufman stadium.

On one of the golf days, George had a conflict and couldn't play. That morning Dave Broderick, one of Brett's close friends, hosted Fred! Dave an excellent player and another Wolf Creek member and outstanding player Ron Brewer made up the threesome. The three would start the round and a fourth, very talented, Creek member John Sinovic would join them on the back nine.

Sinovic was a stick! He was the first Kansas University golfer to make the NCAA Division I All American team and had won the Kansas Amateur Championship. John was contemplating turning professional and had some lofty goals. How would he measure up to PGA Tour star Fred Couples?

Fred Couples

Broderick, Brewer, and Fred Couples finished the front nine and took a break. John Sinovic had arrived, and the kids loaded John's clubs on Brewer's cart. Off they go on hole number 10 and I'm not sure, but I think there might have been a little game set up. Maybe cart against cart! On the Par 5 14th hole all three "Creek" members hit good drives and great lay-up position second shots, leaving each 80-110 yards to the hole. The hole has three cross hazards and is challenging and long.

Fred hit his drive in the middle of the fairway.

With 280 yards to the front of the green, he pulls a 4 wood from his bag and prepares to hit. Sinovic, thinking Couples is unaware of the hazard just short of the green, interrupts Freddie's routine. John, being a nice guy, tells Fred of the blind hazard up there. Couples reply "I know I played here yesterday. "

Couples launches this unbelievable shot! Using a traditional 4-wood (wood), leaving the three Wolf Creek guys in disbelief. He calmly puts his bazooka back in his bag. Sinovic says to Brewer: "that's impossible, I couldn't hit that shot in a hundred years"

As John was getting back in the cart, he said; "Hell, why would I want to play professional golf?"

John Sinovic had just seen and received enough information to decide his future!

Sometimes decisions are Easy! Thank you Boom Boom!

Karsten Comes to Kansas!

Spring in the Metropolitan PGA Section is especially exciting. The golf season is about to begin, and the Pro-Assistant tournament kicks it off. The Spring business and education meeting is held at the famous Westchester Country Club.

It's 1973 and I'm attending my first Spring meeting in the golf business. This is my first look at the PGA inside and boy I'm excited. The "Met" Section prides itself on doing all it does with excellence.

Karsten Solheim

The main speaker for the education portion is a gentleman from Arizona and the founder of PING golf. Karsten Solheim is going to share, with almost 300 of us, his story and specifically tell us about the Lost Wax process and how golf club heads are being cast rather than forged. After his presentation, a panel of 4 "Met" section PGA professionals would interview him.

The program was an unbelievable experience for a young entry-level PGA apprentice. During a break I was able to say hello and shake the hand of Mr. Solheim.

Almost 20 years later March 30, 1982, the Wolf Creek Golf Club, in Olathe Kansas, clubhouse burns to the ground. All contents are lost and nothing, but rubble, twisted steel, and ash remain. What a way to begin my second year as the Golf Director at the Club!

The most popular clubs at Wolf Creek were PINGS and with only 210 members I estimated well over 100 sets were destroyed. In 1982 Ping clubs were allocated and an account could only purchase 5 sets per month. This was not going to work for Wolf Creek or me. I acted and called Arizona (PING) and asked to speak to Mr. Solheim. I was connected, to my surprise, and explained my situation. Karsten offered a solution and asked I send some photos of the fire and they (PING) would research the history between Ping, and the accounts of my predecessor John Bonella, and I.

After just a couple of days, I heard back from Ping and they allowed me to purchase 25 sets a week for 4 weeks. I paid them weekly and everyone was happy!

A few years later, I was tasked with the job as the Education Director for the Midwest PGA Section and we needed a speaker for our Spring education meeting. I reached out to Karsten's secretary and explained who I was and asked if Mr. Solheim would come to Kansas City to speak to our section professionals.

He said "Yes" and did a great talk. He remembered the fire and the PING solution!

What a fantastic contribution Mr. Solheim and his family have made to our great game and golf professionals like me.

Fire

The operator breaks in and interrupts my home phone call! It's 11:15 Monday morning March 30th, 1982. I hear these words: "the fire alarm has gone off at Wolf Creek Golf Club! Instantly my adrenalin spiked. I holler to Cathy:" I'm going to the club, not sure what's happening! Maybe fire!"

I jumped in the Toyota turned south on Antioch Road, go up the hill to 119th Street and see the impossible. Nine miles away, I see a column of black smoke billowing straight up into the Kansas blue sky.

I was hired and started my Kansas golf career at Wolf Creek in February of 1981. My first year at the Creek, as the club's GM/Golf director, had been a great experience. I had gotten to know almost all the 220 members and was enjoying the club's pure golf philosophy! What a great place!

Financially, the club exceeded all my expectations. The members loved golf, enjoyed lessons, supported their golf pro, liked to purchase the most up to date equipment and golf apparel. My golf shop had more than most! I was the first in greater Kansas City to carry Polo and Reebok. We sold Corbin suits, sports coats, Countess Mara ties, Cole Hahn shoes, designer belts, and even personally hemmed or cuffed trousers while our golfers played!

My entire profit from my first year was on the golf shop floor in paid-up inventory as well as much of my Spring purchases not yet paid for.

On that beautiful March morning after speeding thru south Johnson County, I arrived at the club! Witnessing the massive flames and smoke I couldn't believe my eyes. The rural fire department was on-site with 3 or 4 trucks, but they were helpless. There were no hydrants nearby and water was being hauled in a truck from a quarter-mile away! The Kansas Spring wind had picked up and the wood frame building was roaring with fire. A small crowd had gathered and together we watched as the windows implode and heard the terrible sound of the clubs 60 brand new EZ Go golf carts exploding in the basement. There was no way to save the building or any of the contents. The clubhouse would burn to the ground in 24 hours and smolder for days.

Sometimes things go wrong, and this was sure one of those days!

My initial thoughts and reactions were negative and overwhelming! Everything is gone! I felt helpless, scared, frustrated, confused, and defeated.

At about 2:00 pm reality set in! The club president and all the board had been notified, the metro newspapers (Kansas City Star, Overland Park Sun), as well as all 3 KC television stations, were there to report. Wolf Creek fire would be the lead story on the six o'clock news and front-page headline of the papers Tuesday morning.

My mindset had shifted! How could we be open for play in 18 hours? The challenges were enormous! We had lost everything!

For golf, we needed to prioritize and get the basics. We had no golf carts, no members golf clubs in storage, no shoes or member locker contents, no bookkeeping office or records, no food or beverage operation, no range balls, and all my golf shop inventory, antiques, and memorabilia were gone. Imagine, we didn't even have a wooden tee, a scorecard, or a pencil!

Things began to happen! A small construction trailer showed up and was secured in place. EZ Go arranged to have 40 gas golf carts on-site at 7:30 am Tuesday! The nearby golf professionals stepped up and provided some basics. They had range balls, golf gloves, tees, pencils, and other basics dropped off at my home that evening. The president of the club appointed a building committee and a board member to work with our insurance carrier and agent.

That night I got home at about 7:00 PM and planned to watch the 1982 NCAA Basketball finals. A classic game North Carolina versus Georgetown! With no record option on the TV, in the early '80s, and being on the phone, I missed most of the game! The game ended with a last-second Carolina win and was a silver lining on a very dark day! Go "Tarheels!"

At 5:00 AM I met with a member, Wayne Bower, at his home, and we drafted a letter to the membership and included a form to enable the member to list items they had lost in the fire! This proved to be very helpful and could be used for insurance and pricing the cost of replacing lost equipment. Envelopes were hand addressed and the mailing sent that Tuesday morning.

I had found a scorecard, contacted a member who owned a printing company, and was able to copy and print. He had 2000 scorecards to me by 9:00 AM Tuesday.

While the clubhouse smoldered, on Tuesday, March 31st we opened for play! How we did it still boggles my mind!

So many people stepped up and made it happen! Unbelievable!

April 1st, 1982 the fun stuff began! The membership rallied and made the adventure of the 1982 golf season work!

We received a permit to have a double-wide trailer, on-site, to serve as a temporary clubhouse. Electricity, telephone, water, and septic were hooked up! We now had a mini-golf shop and snack bar. With a grill, refrigerator, and freezer added, we were able to have cookouts (lunches) 6 days a week.

The building committee went to work, interviewed, and hired an architect. With plans in place, bids were sought and within a couple of months, the club had our general contractor.

The club's insurance company and the agent made the claim process flow smoothly. Our coverage was very good, and we now had an opportunity to add some floorplan changes that would help with operational efficiency.

My business boomed! Most members wanted to purchase their new equipment from me. The response to the mailing and inventory form was remarkable. The golf staff would receive and price 25-50 forms a day! We coordinated with 12 of the area golf sales representatives and positioned their display vans creating a golf shopping mall!

We sold almost 200 pairs of Footjoy shoes in one day!

One sales representative drove to Pocahontas Arkansas, rented a trailer, and brought us back 80 golf bags!

Ping shipped us 25 sets of irons a week for 4 consecutive weeks as well as putters and woods.

The 1982 season at the Creek was a great success and all major club events were held. The Member-Guest (Timberwolf Classic), Club Championship, and Invitational all went off without a hitch! We even conducted our junior summer camp!

In March of 1983, the new clubhouse opened, and we were back in business.

There is no doubt, in my mind, that any group would have better handled the situation than the Wolf Creek family! This was a model in crisis management. The membership, staff, golf companies, contractors, building committee, and the Wolf Creek Board of Directors did a remarkable job!

I love Wolf Creek!

Chitlin' Switch, Georgia

The wind is out of the North, it's 20 degrees, snowing sideways, and the normal 25-minute drive from my home to Kansas Cities Downtown airport has taken well over an hour. I park the car, fighting the north wind, and trying to stay on my feet, walk to the Executive Air terminal. Waiting inside are the other three members of our foursome.

Our carry-on bags are loaded, and we board the awaiting Falcon jet. Buckled in, we taxied out to the runway and in a flash, we are in the air and above the snow and clouds. The thousand-mile flight to Valdosta Georgia takes just under 2 hours!

In Valdosta a Suburban meets us on the tarmac, baggage is transferred and off we go!

This may sound like the start of a great golf trip, but it is the start of something very different for me!

The foursome is George Brett, Tony Adams, Dave Owen, and Wolf Creek Golf Club's, Golf Professional, me (Jeff Burey)!

George Brett and Tony Adams

We are on our way to "Chitlin' Switch", a plantation owned by Jackson T. Stephens from Little Rock, Arkansas. We were going to hunt some birds.

At the time Jack Stephens was the chairman at a club in the Eastern part of Georgia called Augusta National. Stephens and his brother W.R. "Witt" had built one of the most successful privately-owned companies (Stephens Inc.) in the country. Jack Stephens, a legend, was planning to meet us at the plantation. Raymond Floyd had hunted with Stephens just a couple of days before our trip!

Jeff Burey had only once fired a shotgun, never ridden a horse, only hunted with a slingshot as a kid and to this day I don't know why I was included on this safari.

For me, this trip would be equivalent to, your first baseball experience being World Series game seven at Yankee stadium, or your first pro football game the Super Bowl, or your first college basketball game UNC at Duke. If you liked to hunt, this experience would equal any of those!

George, Tony, and Dave had quite a bit in common! All were Wolf Creek members, loved golf, great athletes, friends, and loved to hunt. These guys excelled at whatever they attempted.

Tony Adams, football quarterback played 3 years at Utah State University and professional football for almost a decade. Adams played in the World, Canadian, and National Football Leagues. Tony played for the Kansas City Chiefs from 1975-1978. Adams excelled at all the sports and was an expert hunter and fisherman. Tony had a very good golf game and loved to play.

George Brett, Kansas City Royal professional baseball Hall of Famer played his entire 20-year career in K.C. The 1985 World Series champion, the major league All-Star and American League batting champion in 3 decades, Brett was the face of Royals baseball! George was also an avid golfer and played whenever possible. Brett was an experienced outdoorsman and would hunt with Adams.

Dave Owen had organized this trip and there may have been more than bird hunting in mind! The Stephens' jet, timing, Brett meeting Jack Stephens, what's up?

Owen had been Kansas Lieutenant Governor, was a very successful entrepreneur, and, working with Stephens Inc. Dave lived

The "Hack"

nearby Wolf Creek, had a beautiful ranch, and was a regular on the rodeo circuit. Dave and I would often play a late afternoon 9-holes of golf at the "Creek."

The Suburban turned off the country highway and we approached the Plantation house. The longleaf pines were everywhere, and the house reminded me of the Augusta clubhouse, only much smaller. The white structure with black shutters fits in perfectly. A stable, dog kennel and skeet /trap range nearby made for a beautiful and peaceful setting.

After moving into our rooms, it was now evening and time for dinner! Two wonderful ladies greeted us and prepared a fabulous Southern meal, (Biscuits, gravy, fried chicken, cornbread, collards, green beans, corn on the cob, okra, with Sweet tea and peach cobbler for dessert)

With dinner finished we played a little Gin rummy and I could only imagine what was in store for the morning!

It's 6:30 and I wake up to the smell of bacon and ham grilling on the stove. George Brett is in the kitchen with the ladies thinking he's helping prepare breakfast! Showered and ready I notice our boots polished, shotguns oiled, and the sun is shining through the pines.

Breakfast grits, biscuits with homemade butter, jam, eggs to order, hash brown potatoes, and the best sausage, ham, and bacon I have ever had!

After breakfast, I was ready to go back to bed, but the day was only about to begin. We met the dog handler Frank and went to warm up by shooting some clays. Fun for me to watch and I even fired a shot. I was coached a little but not very proficient! My shot was nowhere near the clay, but the clay was destroyed as Tony Adams was my back-up!

Down the road came a mule-drawn Hack, a wagon with an elderly gentleman at the reins with a bird dog on the seat next to him. On the back of the Hack were 4 kennels with 4 pairs of German Shorthair bird dogs. These were working dogs! Behind the Hack, with reins attached, were 4 saddled Tennessee Walking horses for us!

We were introduced to the driver and our horses! Of course, my horse was Mr. Stephen's mount! I was told his name was Lightning. Did I mention I had never ridden a horse!

I put my shotgun in the holster that was attached to the saddle and carefully climbed up on Lightning's back, grabbed the reins, and let this beautiful animal lead me! Lightning made it easy and I went along for the ride!

After riding about a quarter of a mile in the piney forest, 1 pair of dogs was released from a kennel on the Hack. They went to work and in just a few minutes went on Point. We dismounted, grabbed our shotguns from the holsters, and were ready. A covey exploded and bang, bang, bang! Tony, George, and Dave had each shot a bird! I was in awe just watching!

The old dog on the seat of the Hack was tasked with retrieving the birds and did!

They hunted until about 1:00 and returned to the house for a great lunch and a rest. Back out to hunt at about 2:30 and we returned to the house at about 4:30. On the way back Dave decided they would race back! The three took off and Lightning had to follow! I wasn't sure I would ever see Kansas again! My heart was pounding!

Back at the house, I asked if there were any fish in the lake and the next thing to appear were four fishing poles. To the lake, we went! Tony, George, and Dave went out in the Bass boat and I stayed onshore. Brett caught the same fish 3 times.

Back at the house, we learned that Jack Stephens had a conflict and would not be coming for dinner, but John Schuerholz, General Manager of the Atlanta Braves, and former Royals GM would be coming.

One more great evening and dinner. Brett and Schuerholz had a good visit!

Back to Valdosta and on to KC in the morning! Wow! What a trip!

I think the trip to Chitln' Switch was set up for Jack Stephens to meet George Brett and possibly make an offer to purchase the Kansas City Royals.

I do know I rode a horse, fired a shotgun, didn't catch a fish, probably never shot a bird, and had an amazing trip to Georgia!

Dave Owen

My Friend the Artist

I met John Martin shortly after moving to Kansas and we have been friends for almost 40 years. John and his wife Bonnie are fabulous people and they both have amazing artistic and creative talent! It has been a great experience to watch as he has done so many wonderful works of art!

John Boyd Martin is a lifelong Kansan and was born and raised in Ottawa. He is a proud graduate of the University of Kansas and the School of Fine Arts.

John started his career as a graphic designer and illustrator. He then became an advertising art director and has earned more than 150 local and national awards! In 1986 he decided to use his creativity and talent to pursue his first true love, Portraiture.

John Martin Pencil Our three kids!

As one of the most accomplished portrait artists in America, his paintings are a treasure.

John's work in collegiate and professional sport is legendary and his golf work is extra special to me. He has painted numerous professional golfers and always does it with perfection. John has painted Palmer, Nicklaus, Watson, Floyd, Trevino, and many more.

Lee Trevino

John Martin has supported me and has contributed so much to help me try to grow the game of golf. John's enthusiasm, encouragement, and friendship have been something I will always be thankful for. John Boyd Martin, you are a great friend!

Young Tom Watson

Arnold Palmer "The King"

Jack Nicklaus "Old Tom Morris" Award

Dean Smith, UNC

"Never Say Never!"

I had the privilege to work 27 years as a golf professional and General Manager at Wolf Creek in Olathe Kansas. I enjoyed the opportunity to take groups of members on golf trips! We would travel almost anywhere warm in the early Spring, late fall, and winter. North Carolina, Florida, Arizona, Texas, and California were the states we most traveled.

Most years I tried to make a trip in April with 3 members, play golf in Atlanta, Charlotte, or Columbia, South Carolina. On Monday of Masters week, we would go to the practice round at Augusta. Tickets were available, crowds smaller, players relaxed, and you could get up close to them. We would make memories for sure!

To say the very least, Wolf Creek had some members with interesting personalities. Most were, direct, confident, experts, successful and great to learn from. A few of our guys had very strong opinions and never seemed hesitant to express them.

Magnolia Lane, Augusta

Dr. Charles Everson

Dr. Charles Everson was a good guy, an excellent dentist, (endodontist)specializing in root canals. Doc Everson was my fifth of fourteen presidents during my tenure at the Creek ! Charlie loved Wolf Creek, his golf at the Landmark Properties in Palm Desert, and other destination courses. Everson had never been to Augusta!

Charlie Everson would have been the Gold Medal winner had there been a prize for the Most Opinionated. He had opinions about politics, sports, automobiles, and golf course trees. There was never a question as to what the Doc thought!

I had two doctor friends who were cardiologists' in Augusta. Many Augusta kids had come to our summer camp when I was at Pinehurst. Dr. Harry Harper the Augusta National member and Dr. Weems Pennington were partners in their medical practice. I was invited four times to bring another player and make a two and a half day trip to play Augusta National.

I had gone twice and asked Charlie Everson if he would like to go with me on this third visit? Doc said yes and we booked a March trip (Thursday, Friday and Saturday) for the two of us.

We flew to Atlanta on Thursday morning, got our car, and played Atlanta Athletic club. We spent the night in Atlanta and Friday morning, we made the two-hour drive to Augusta. At 10 minutes to noon, we arrived at the main gate! Looking down the Magnolia lane, which never gets old, the security guard approached and said: "Dr. Harper was on the property." He welcomed us and directed us to the parking.

We met and I introduced Charlie to the Augusta doctors! We had a nice lunch and brought our overnight bags in and went down to our assigned rooms below the Golf shop. Dr. Harper took us to the locker room to change shoes. We were assigned caddies and went to the practice area which was then north of Magnolia drive.

Our round was very enjoyable, and the three doctors had good chemistry. I know Charlie Everson was thrilled, and I remember the seven iron he hit 15 feet from the hole on the 12th hole.

Dr. Harper knew all the Augusta National history and gave us an unbelievable tour. He was as informative as any museum Docent! We saw Augusta from top to bottom! We went up to the Crow's Nest, the Champions locker room, the Par three, the cottages, and saw the famous wisteria on the backside of the clubhouse.

On many occasions, I've heard Charlie Everson say: "When my daughter got married that would be the last time! I won't ever wear a tie again! Never will I wear a tie again! I will never wear a tie again! I've thrown away all my ties so I will never have to wear one again! I'm done with ties and never will need one again!" He meant it!

Augusta Clubhouse

So, after showering and dressing for dinner, Dr. Harper asks if we are ready and reminds us about wearing a tie. Now, this is interesting for me to see the KC Doc's response. What I thought was impossible happened! Charlie without hesitating says: "I didn't bring a tie, where can I get one?" A tie is magically delivered! Wearing our ties, we go upstairs and have a great dinner. Augusta National has an enchanting effect on us all!

Saturday morning, we have breakfast, hit some warmup balls, play our second round, have lunch and it's back to Atlanta and Delta to Kansas City!

I can't imagine a better experience and Doc Everson was thrilled!

Charlie had told lots of stories about our trip to Georgia, but didn't to the best of my knowledge, nor do I ever remember him telling about having to wear a tie at that Friday night Augusta National dinner!

So, remember: "Never say Never!"

Augusta Champions Locker Room

"Sawbones"

Wolf Creek Golf Club in Olathe Kansas is where I spent over 26 years as the General Manager/ Golf Professional. The Creek is in south Johnson County, about 19 miles south of Kansas City. What a place!

The membership is very special and the main reason to be a member at the Creek is and will always be GOLF! No other amenities are needed!

Unique in many ways, Wolf Creek has a limited membership, no tee times, fantastic layout, fast play, always in great condition and this club sets the standard for fast and true greens.

I can't imagine a better place to have spent most of my professional career. The memories, people, and experiences at the Creek are priceless. I think I could write 100 stories about Wolf Creek, its members, and fun history.

One of the unique things about Wolf Creek is that most members would have a nickname! We had Monkey, Booby, Peaches, Tree, Dr. Bazaar, Raymar, Turkey, Viking, Bucket Mouth, Helmet Head, Midnight, Tin Head, Moo, Diet Coke, Tinkerbell, Spud, PODC, Miler More, Jumbo and at least 100 more. (some of which I'm not comfortable printing). These nicknames often had something to do with the member's profession, appearance, an incident, or personality.

Dr. Donald "Sawbones" Piper

One of my favorite members (not supposed to have favorites) was Dr. Don Piper, Doc was a longtime orthopedic surgeon and like all members at the Creek loved the game. Doc was a lanky, witty, great guy and appropriately nicknamed Sawbones. Piper, a lifelong golfer had been a member at Hillcrest CC in Kansas City (Donald Ross Course) for over 20 years and joined Wolf Creek early in the '70s. In his day Doc was a pretty good player, but like all of us, as he aged, his golf game became more challenging. Sawbones was always striving to maintain the skills he still had and find some skills he had lost along the way!

One day Doc was on the putting green practicing very short putts. He had a very severe case of the yips and he couldn't hit the hole. One of the great old KC golf professionals, Buster Mills, approached the Doc, and after witnessing an 18-inch putt miss the hole 4 inches to the right had to ask, "Doc what do you think about when you take the putter back?" Sawbones calmly replied "Suicide."

Another day the old Doc and I were playing and on the par 4,12th hole, he hit his best drive of the day. He had a soft 9 iron to the hole and looking confident hit probably one of the worst shots ever. Doc had hit a cold shank straight right into Wolf Creek. Sawbones, without emotion, put his 9-iron back in his bag, crossed his arms, looked skyward, and said "Beam me up, Scotty"

Oh boy, did Wolf Creek have some memorable characters!

The Masters Champion

On April 9, 1967, Gay Robert Brewer Jr. won the Masters! Brewer posted a 72-hole score of 280 to defeat Bobby Nichols by one shot. This was the highlight of his exceptional professional career. Gay's accomplishments included 10 PGA Tour wins, 1 PGA Senior Tour win, and as a member of the team, winning the 1967 Ryder Cup.

Gay Brewer was born in Middleton, Ohio, and raised in Lexington, Kentucky. In 1949 he won the US Junior Amateur and in 1952 won the Southern Amateur.

I met Gay Brewer twice!

1967 was one of the most memorable years of my life. 67 was my senior year of high school graduating in June. I played on our Norwalk (Connecticut) High School basketball team that had to follow our 1966 Connecticut State Championship team. We exceeded most everyone's expectations by winning the East division of our conference and playing two rounds in the State Tournament.

Gay Brewer, 1967 Masters Champion

Playing golf was my passion and although I worked as a caddy and on the grounds crew at Shorehaven Golf Club I loved to compete. I played on the high school golf team, had a good season, and won all my eight matches at our home course, Shorehaven. I played every junior tournament possible in 1967. I qualified for the Metropolitan Golf Association Junior, Westchester Junior, Connecticut State Junior (Losing in the semifinals), state Jaycee Junior, and represented Connecticut in the New England Junior Team Championship at Essex County Club in Massachusetts. I was motivated and maybe even fanatical.

The first time I met Gay Brewer was that summer in 1967!

It was the end of August and the Westchester Country Club was hosting the very first Westchester Classic. (Jack Nicklaus won) This was a big deal for the New York Metropolitan area.

Member Clubs of the Westchester Golf Association were asked to recruit volunteers to forecaddie and marshal specific holes for a day. I wasn't a member of a club but was invited by a good golfing friend Andy Banfield, whose family were members at the nearby Silvermine Golf Club. I was thrilled and was going to my first tour event.

The players competing were the very best, and everyone was excited because Arnie and Jack were playing. Our assignment on day # 2 (second round) was, I think, hole number 12. Wow, I get to spend the day, with a pole and flag, spotting and marking tee shots being hit by the greatest players in the world.

Most of the players would hit their drives in the fairway, their second shot, and move on. You always knew where Arnold Palmer was because the roar of the big army told you. I had a Pairing sheet, so I could tell who was about to come thru. Up comes Masters Champion Gay Brewer's group to our hole, my heart was racing. I'm excited. I could tell he is about to hit his drive and I had my caddie eyes locked in.

Brewer swings, the ball looks like it's right down the middle, and then it dives left and enters the dense woods. Not good! He was the last to hit, I'm in the right rough, and I take off running across the fairway and into the woods. I'm excited because I spotted the ball immediately and was in position waiting, with my pole, for the

NAME OF GOLF HOLES	
1	Tea Olive
2	Pink Dogwood
3	Flowering Peach
4	Flowering Crabapple
5	Magnolia
6	Juniper
7	Pampas
8	Yellow Jasmine
9	Carolina Cherry
10	Camerlia
11	White Dogwood
12	Golden Bell
13	Azalea
14	Chinese Fir
15	Fire Thorn
16	Red Bud
17	Nandina
18	Holly

Gay Brewer
1967

AUGUSTA
NATIONAL
GOLF
CLUB

Masters champion Gay Brewer to arrive. First came the caddie and then Brewer. Masters Champ says: "Kid is that my ball?" Answer: "Yes Sir!" Question: "Did you put it there?" Answer: "No Sir!" The Masters' Champ chops it out to the fairway and is gone. I had met Gay Brewer for the first time!

He missed the cut!

The second time and last time I met Gay Brewer was at Wolf Creek Golf Club in Olathe Kansas. The tradition was, if there wasn't a Monday Section tournament, a few of the local club professionals, would make a game and play at one of our clubs. The Monday game was informal but great fun! I didn't play very often but loved it when we played at my club, Wolf Creek.

Sometime in the summer of 1984 PGA professional Randy Towner put together a game with eight of us. (Geoff Hensley, Brad Sater, Randy, me, and probably Stan Thirsk, Charles Lewis, and Bud Williamson). One of the others also had invited Gay Brewer to make the eighth. Randy threw the eight balls into the air and my Titleist lands closest to Gay Brewer. We were partners and rode the cart together for 18 holes. This guy was competitive still, so encouraging, engaging, and fun. I had an awesome and memorable day with Gay Brewer! Somewhere during the round, I told the Masters Champion of 1967, I had met him in 67. He asked where and I said "Westchester." He looked at me and said, "that was not a good week and all I wanted was to get out of New York and go home!"

Gay Brewer's wife Carole Lee had grown up in Kansas and they lived in Mission Hills from about 1983 to 1988. Not long after Carole Lee died in 1988, Brewer moved to Florida and maintained a summer place in Lexington.

I figure I spent about four hours and three minutes with the 1967 Masters Champion. The Kid from Connecticut enjoyed four hours in Kansas much more than the three minutes in New York.

I thought the 1967 Masters Champion was a nice guy!

Gay Brewer died in August of 2007.

Wolf Creek Hole #11

The "Umpire" Strikes Back

Most Golf Clubs/ Country Clubs have some very interesting and amazing members. Wolf Creek Golf Club in Olathe Kansas was no exception. The Creek Opened in 1971 and from day one has attracted fantastic members.

Wolf Creek members come from all walks of life. The club had bankers, doctors, dentists, lawyers, small business folks, corporate executives, restauranteurs, contractors of all kinds, airline pilots, and more. As the Creek's PGA professional I often have said, "I don't have all the answers, but I have the contacts to usually find the answer."

Professional athletes, coaches, and people in the sporting world made up a significant percentage of the Wolf Creek membership. The club, from the NFL, had guys named Marty, Marcus, and Carlos. From MLB had Ewing, George, Buddy, and David. From the PGA tour, there was Tom, Matt, Woody, Jim, and another Tom.

One of the members from Major League Baseball was Stephen M. Palermo. Steve was the model for what a Major League umpire might be! His reputation was stellar.

Steve Palermo

Palermo joined Wolf Creek in the mid to late '80s. He loved playing golf at the Creek and had a pretty good game. His personality was dynamic, and Stevie was probably one of the most engaging Storytellers.

Being New Englanders, living in Kansas, almost the same age, Stevie and I had much in common and often shared stories.

July 7th, 1991 was a horrible dark day for Steve, his family, baseball, and all Stevie's friends at Wolf Creek. Palermo had umpired a Texas Ranger night game, had dinner, and was leaving when he encountered a situation where two waitresses were being mugged in the parking lot. Steve confronted the assailants and was shot. The bullet grazed his spinal cord and he was instantly paralyzed below the waist. Doctors told Steve and his wife Debbie that he would probably never walk again. All of us witnessed Steve's determination, his experiencing multiple surgeries, and his phenomenal rehabilitation. Walking using one small leg brace and a cane, Steve managed to walk again.

Wolf Creek Hole #11

In 1998 Steve rejoined Wolf Creek, determined to play golf again and he did.

Wolf Creek had a Captain of Golf. Capt. Bill Middleton was at the club almost every day and one of Stevie's many friends. Steve again was not to be denied and practiced and played a few holes a couple of times a week.

On one morning Capt. Bill and Steve teed off Hole # 10 and planned to play 3 or 4 holes (Steve now had his specially designed golf cart). The twosome got to the 11th hole, the most difficult par 3 on the course. From the up-tee Palermo tops his shot into the gunch. He tees up a second ball and knocks it in the hole.

Hole in One?

I say "Yes!"

Debbie Palermo recently told me Steve had made three "Holes in One" before the Texas incident.

Stephen Palermo died on May 14, 2017.

Anyone who had the opportunity to meet or know Steve Palermo was truly blessed!

The "Umpire Struck Back!"

STEVE PALERMO
1949-2017

Barbecue and Golf with a Billionaire

Kansas City is known for its incredible barbecue and the area has no shortage of great restaurants. There are over 100! Many of the KC barbecue sauces are sold throughout the country.

It didn't take long after moving to Overland Park Kansas in 1981 for Cathy and me to discover what a treat a barbecue dinner was. KC barbecue is a way of life here and everyone seems to have a favorite restaurant.

The Golf Professional position at Wolf Creek Golf Club brought us to Kansas in 1981 and I knew very little about anything midwestern. I soon learned that only Rome has more fountains and Paris more boulevards than Kansas City. The beautiful Country Club Plaza located just south of downtown was the first drive to shopping area and was constructed in 1922. The home and presidential library of Harry S. Truman our 33rd president is in nearby Independence. The corporate home of Sprint and Hallmark are here. The Disney family moved to town when Walt was 9 years old! Disney grew up in Kansas City and Mickey Mouse was conceived here before Walt moved him to California. Kansas City has three major sports franchises: The Royals, the Chiefs, and Tom Watson!

Art Williams

My former boss, mentor, and friend is a guy named Lou Miller. Lou is one of the most dynamic individuals on the planet and has positively impacted many hundreds of lives and mine especially. Miller hired me at Pinehurst, where I had lived and worked before coming to Kansas.

Lou grew up in Georgia and loved all sports, especially football! He attended Presbyterian College in Clinton South Carolina and played football there. Lou's teammate and the Presbyterian quarterback was Arthur L. "Art" Williams Jr. Also, from Georgia, Art and Lou soon became friends. Art Williams transferred to Mississippi State where he also played QB and graduated. Williams earned his master's degree at Auburn. From his days in high school Art always wanted to be a professional football coach and no doubt would have been very successful!

Lou Miller coached 4 years of high school football in Georgia with Art Williams before both had gigantic career changes! Lou entered the golf business and Art the insurance industry. In February of 1977, along with 85 others, Art founded his own company. A. L. Williams & Associates (now Primerica). With over 100,000 agents became the largest seller of Life insurance in the United States. In professional sports, Art owned the National Hockey League's Tampa Bay Lightning and the Canadian Football League's Birmingham Barracudas! Many wise investments also added to Williams wealth.

Miller a golf professional and Williams a golfer often worked on the practice tee and played together! In discussing destination golf and having seen a recent article in Golf Digest, Lou suggested a trip to the Sandhills Golf Club in Mullen Nebraska. Lou said to Art: "You provide the transportation and I will take care of the rest!"

The planning began to take shape. Being a member at Sandhills I could host 7 guests for this 2-day overnight golf experience. Dates set, cabin accommodations arranged, Art and Lou invited 5 other Georgia/ Florida golfing friends.

Saying Art would provide the transportation is an understatement! Art had just purchased a brand-new Gulfstream 4 Jet and this trip would be its maiden flight. The group would fly from Augusta Georgia and pick me up at Johnson County Kansas Executive Airport just one mile from my home and then off to the western Nebraska Sandhills.

The day the trip began was a Sunday morning and I watched as the beautiful aircraft glided in for a perfect landing. The plane taxied in and the cabin door opened and out comes Lou Miller. The other 6 gentlemen follow, and Lou introduces me. After a 10 minute stretch break my clubs and overnight bag are loaded. Buckled in, out to the runway, and off to North Platte Nebraska we go! The 400-mile flight was seamless!

We landed and with 2 minivans waiting on the tarmac. Our golf and overnight bags are loaded. The one-hour 65-mile drive is one of my favorite parts of the Sandhills experience. The drive takes you thru the little town of Tryon and north toward Mullen. This is cattle ranch country and the rolling terrain with sand blowouts is spectacular and makes for interesting conversation. You can drive a ten-mile stretch and see possibly a single-vehicle, most likely a pick-up truck, and the drivers almost always wave. As you approach the winding entrance and 2 to 3-mile drive to the clubhouse, you first must cross the Dismal river. This is my reminder to be ready for the entrance. I have mistakenly driven past more than once.

As we approach the clubhouse and lodges it is easy to be underwhelmed, but now the Sandhills experience kicks in! Greeted by a smile and a Husker hello our golf bags are loaded on carts. The baggage is taken to the assigned cabins, which are in the only wooded area, in the valley, and back-up to the Dismal River.

We enter the clubhouse, register, check out the golf shop and make the mile or so, winding golf cart drive to the golf course and Ben's porch (as in Crenshaw). The porch serves as the halfway house and Starters Perch.

Sand Hills Hole #18

After a short stop at the warm-up driving range, we approach the highest spot on the 8000-acre property. It is a spectacular view, and you can see for miles. The first look at this Coore/Crenshaw masterpiece is unbelievable and thoroughly breathtaking. The big blue sky, beautiful contrast of the green firm fairways, with native grasses and awesome natural blow-out bunkers has the look and feel of an Irish seaside course. There must be an ocean or sea just over the dunes.

Two foursomes assigned, my group takes the lead and my cart partner is Art Williams. Lou Miller played in the second group! I'm in my element! What could be better, answering questions, telling stories, playing golf with a nice guy, on one of the best and most unique golf courses in the world.

After 9 holes we have an extraordinary Nebraska beef burger at the Porch and then play the back 9. Having enough daylight, we play an extra 9.

We head back to the clubhouse, drop off our clubs, and walk down to our 4 cabins. After a shower and short rest, we meet at the clubhouse for another favorite part of the Sandhills experience. Where are we? The appetizers and dinners are out of this world. The local western Nebraska beef is as good as it gets! I love listening to the stories as the group recaps the full afternoon of golf! I will always hear comments about the firmness and speed of the greens. This group had 2 Augusta members and they concurred.

Wow! What a first day!

Day two starts with a traditional Sandhills breakfast, new stories, and the anticipation of 18 more holes. Our clubs are loaded, we hit a few balls to warm-up, roll some practice putts, and head to the first tee. The wind has changed direction and the golf course is 180 degrees different! It is unique to Sandhills that the scorecard does not include the handicaps of the individual holes. The wind can blow from any direction. I have never seen this, nor had anyone else in the group.

9 holes, again lunch at the Porch and the final 9.

Sadly, with golf complete, we pack, load-up the vans and it's back to North Platte and a trip home with one more stop in Kansas!

The G-4 again lands at Johnson County Executive and Cathy was waiting on the tarmac with our minivan and sedan. The weary golfers deplane and load up and make the 3-minute drive to our home. A traditional KC barbecue dinner was ready! Ribs, brisket, burnt ends, and onion rings from Fiorella's Jack Stack Barbecue restaurant. Cathy's homemade potato salad and coleslaw are a hit! Full, back to the airport, and ready for a nap, goodbyes are exchanged. The Gulfstream 4 taxies out and dramatically takes off for Augusta with the seven southern gentlemen!

The Sandhills experience is always fun and it is a pleasure to host! The Sandhill's staff from Mullen and Hooker county are gracious, forthright, and truly are a highlight of the trip! Nebraska has a mystique all its own and is evident in the pride of its people.

The billionaire, Art Williams and the group had a bucket list experience and one we will never forget!

Sand Hills Hole #18

Rock Star for a Day

The US Women's Open Championship conducted by the United States Golf Association is the premier women's golf championship in the world. The Women's Open is contested on some of the finest golf courses America has to offer.

The first week of July 2002, Prairie Dunes Country Club in Hutchinson, Kansas, hosted the Open. LPGA star Julie Inkster won the Championship and the Dunes, designed and built by Perry and Press Maxwell proved to be a fantastic venue.

My story goes something like this:

In mid-winter (2001-2002) I received a phone call from Betse Hamilton. Betse was the USGA's Championship Director for the Women's Open. We had worked together at Pinehurst, where she had been our tournament director. I was on staff and Head golf professional and I had a front-row seat and watched Betse at work. This lady knew her stuff, managed all tournaments at Pinehurst, and always did this gigantic job with excellence.

Betse's call included a request and I'm always willing to help. She explained it had become a tradition the have a local Big Name celebrity conduct a clinic for kids on Tuesday before the Thursday start of the championship. Betse further explained that Michael Jordan had done Chicago and Mia Hamm did Pine Needles, North Carolina the prior two years. Betse asked if I would feel comfortable contacting Roy Williams, Kansas University, head basketball coach. Since I knew Roy quite well, I agreed to call him and ask if he might be available and headline the Tuesday, July 2nd junior clinic.

We hung up and immediately I tried to call Roy. He wasn't available, so I left him a message. Coach called back in just a few minutes and said he would have loved to do it but had a family commitment in South Carolina for the Fourth of July week.

I called Betse and didn't want to disappoint her. Since Roy was out, I suggested I might contact baseball legend, George Brett. Betse was quiet for a few seconds and then asked, "Do you think George Brett might do it?"

I said, "Let me call him, see what he thinks and ask if he is available. I will call you right back."

I dialed Brett's number and he answered. George's first words were: "Jeff, what do you need?" I explained what was planned for July 2nd and of course had to share the Jordan/ Hamm part of the story. He seemed interested, checked his schedule, and agreed to do it.

The call back to my pal Betse was fun! I know she was thrilled and excited to have George. I had a request for her. I said I would like to act as emcee, share a few things with the kids and introduce George Brett. She agreed and we were set.

As July 2nd approached, I had a few details to iron out. I lined out a plane to transport us, from KC to Hutchinson, the day of. I needed

to plan what the clinic might look like and determine where on-site this clinic might take place. I didn't' have a clue as to how many juniors we might have.

I made a trip to Prairie Dunes for planning and Betse found a great spot for the clinic to take place. The on-site tournament management company was to build us a platform/ stage where we would be for the clinic.

On the morning of July 2nd, 2002, we were flown to Hutchinson, greeted by a great group of folks, and had a police escort to the Dunes. I would be with George Brett every step of the way! Everybody knew George, he did a great job with a short press conference, and we had a light lunch. We were escorted out to the clinic site, with 100's of folks wanting to see George Brett.

Clinic Time!

George Brett in action!

At the site, there were 2-3 thousand kids and families waiting for the Hall of Famer George Brett. I got to do a short history lesson and did the introduction of the Kansas City legend. George did a fantastic job and after his clinic signed autographs for almost two hours.

Police escort back to the clubhouse, motorcade to the airport, and back to Kansas City.

George Brett was the talent, July 2nd, but I felt like a "Rock Star" that day!

Postscript

George Brett four years after our clinic was voted the <u>Hometown Hero</u> for the Kansas City Royals in a two-month fan vote. ESPN revealed this honor on the night of September 27, 2006, in an hour-long telecast. Brett received more than 400,000 votes from his fans.

After almost 27 years at Wolf Creek Golf Club, on March 1, 2007, I began my role as General Manager of Prairie Dunes Country Club. What a great opportunity and experience!

Broadway Comes to Prairie Dunes

Located 52 miles west of Wichita is the city of Hutchinson, Kansas. Hutch has a population of just over forty thousand and is the home of the Kansas State Fair. The central Kansas community has the Hutchinson Community College, the fabulous Cosmosphere Space Museum, Underground Salt Mine Museum, a very nice airport, and an outstanding medical community.

Hutchinson is also home to the world-famous Prairie Dunes Country Club.

In the mid-1930s Emerson Carey and his four sons founded the club. Nine original holes were laid-out and put in place by Perry Maxwell. The course opened for play on September 30th, 1937. Twenty years later, an additional nine holes, designed by Perry's son Press Maxwell, were added. The major golf publications consistently recognize Prairie Dunes as one of the Best Courses in the world and always "Number One in Kansas."

The Dunes has hosted many USGA competitions and championships. The US Women's Amateur three times, Curtis Cup, US Mid Am, US Senior Am, as well as two "Majors." The US Women's Open in 1995 and the US Senior Open in 2006. Prairie Dunes has been the site of six Trans-Mississippi Amateurs and six Kansas Golf Association State Amateur championships and so many more collegiate and PGA Section tournaments.

Prairie Dunes Hole #7

Prairie Dunes Hole #2

In January of 2007, I was hired as General Manager at Prairie Dunes. Having been at Wolf Creek in Olathe, Kansas for 27 years, I was very aware of the rich history and unbelievable reputation of the Dunes. Also having been at Wee Burn Country Club in Darien Connecticut and Pinehurst, I had a very real appreciation for golf history, great course architecture, and tradition.

I began my role as General Manager at Prairie Dunes on March 1st and it didn't take me long to confirm some things known, but also to learn some new! I confirmed what a great membership (local and national) Prairie Dunes had in place. Even though I had played the course multiple times, I realized it was even better than I remembered. This world-famous course was special and included all the other amenities expected of a country club. Tennis, swimming, kid's activities, weddings, parties, and meeting rooms were all part of the package.

As a manager, I have always felt the most important priority is to have a clear mission and a great team. Prairie Dunes already had that team in place and was providing a great experience for members and guests, my job was simple: provide these dedicated, loyal, hardworking, professional team members what they needed to do their jobs.

Adam Sabri, the Food and Beverage Director was simply outstanding. Adam came to the Dunes from Ben Hogan's club, Shady Oaks in Texas, and had also worked in Lake Tahoe. Sabri was incredible! He could plan and execute events with ease. When asked a question, Adam's favorite response was "We will make it happen!" Parties, weddings, meetings, holidays, birthdays, kids' events--Sabri

always had them covered.

I watched as Prairie Dunes hosted some of the best and special Members Nights. It was common for Adam to bring in magicians, comedians, and ventriloquists from Las Vegas or Lake Tahoe. He also planned and executed a Renaissance Night featuring characters in costume, authentic food, and included club members as part of the show! We hosted presentations by Golf Digests' Architectural Editor Ron Witten and University of North Carolina-Chapel Hill Psychology Professor and golf author, Dick Coop.

One of my favorite events was when Doug Montgomery, pianist, came to Prairie Dunes. Doug had earned his master's degree from Juilliard School of Music in 1978 and returned to teach in New York for a year. This world-class musician had traveled the country where celebrities, presidents, royalty, ambassadors, and even Arnold and Winnie Palmer became admirers. Montgomery performed in Palm Springs in the winter and Santa Fe in the summer. I had seen Doug in California and Carolyn Dillon (a grand lady and Prairie Dunes member) knew Doug from her summers in New Mexico. Adam and Mrs. Dillon went to work and planned a fabulous evening! Per Montgomery's request, Sabri "made it happen" and secured a Steinway & Sons Grand piano from Wichita State University. Dillon planned an over-the-top dinner menu. The Black-Tie affair wowed the membership. Doug Montgomery demonstrated his wide-ranging talent by playing music from Bach to The Beatles and everything in between. During the intermission, I was humming a Beatles song. Doug asked: "Do you like their music?" I said: "I grew up with it." He began the second part of his performance with a medley of at least a half a dozen Beatle songs.

Adam said: Unbelievable!

What a memorable evening!

Sabri did it again!

He brought Broadway to Prairie Dunes!

Doug Montgomery

Gonzo

Can you imagine, going to the golf course with your best friend almost every day? That's what many hundreds, if not thousands of dogs, get to do. They are up at dawn eagerly anticipating their daily trek to the golf course.

Mark Newton is the Golf Course Superintendent at Canyon Farms Golf Club in Lenexa Kansas. Mark has a dog named "Gonzo." A 3-year-old Australian Shepard, Labrador Retriever mix, Gonzo jumps in the truck with Mark and heads to the golf course.

Golf course superintendents have very demanding jobs! Managing, maintaining, growing great turf is even more difficult in our transition zone. Super's are often subjected to stress and often face situations out of their control.

Golf course dogs, that are always happy, add levity and, camaraderie to the entire turf team!

Kansas City area golf organizations (Midwest PGA Section, Kansas Golf Foundation, Central Links Golf Association, The First Tee of Greater KC, and the Heart of America Golf Course Superintendents) have made a concerted effort to work together and to support and grow the game. An informal alliance of these groups was formed! The goal was to put more: "Footprints in Fairways." Communication/coordination amongst the groups has been awesome.

In the early fall of 2017, I had an idea! I thought, wouldn't it be great to have a golf Calendar that would highlight our local golf organizations under the "Footprints and Fairways" umbrella. I had seen many golf calendars featuring golf course holes and golf art, but my favorites are dog calendars produced by "Big Guys" like the national golf course grounds equipment manufacturers and golf course agricultural and seed product suppliers.

I felt this project would be nothing but positive and it was!

Gaining the approval of the PGA Section Foundation, the Heart of America Golf Course Superintendent's directors, and having the time, I embarked on the project. I was ready to go!

All I needed now was a plan, timetable, budget, printer/ graphic designer, photographer, communication and photo locations, distribution plan, and most of all the talent (the Dogs).

The project timetable was aggressive! We had to have the printing complete and the calendar ready for distribution before the Christmas holiday season.

A Title sponsor emerged! John Deere Golf Equipment, and the local Deere golf dealer, Van Wall Equipment. They took the lead! Sponsors for each of the twelve months stepped up. All the members of the Footprints in Fairways: alliance participated.

The plan in place, with a break-even budget, was completed. The Heart of America office sent a communication out to all the superintendents. If they wanted to have their dog considered, they just needed to return a short questionnaire and photo of their canine.

Twelve Dogs were selected, and the talent was in place. We had a wide range of breeds, Miniature Pinchers to German shepherds. We had "Bruiser, Neema, Fisher, Millie, Harper, Letty, Jacob, Boerne, Ellie, Livie, Frazier and, what would be, the "Cover Dog ", Gonzo,

A fantastic printer was retained, Brian Dibble (Precision Printing, Lenexa Kansas), and did the layouts and graphic design work.

Our Professional Photographer/Producer was special to me. Our daughter Blair Jackson did an incredible job. We confirmed 3 early morning shoots with 4 dogs each. Milburn Country Club Overland Park, Wolf Creek Olathe, and Stone Canyon, Blue Springs Missouri hosted us and the Star dogs. My role for the shoots was to stand behind Blair and squeeze a squeaker to prompt our dogs. Tough duty!

The project was completed on time, on budget, and 5000 free copies distributed throughout the greater Kansas City metro.

These dogs continue to delight!

Bruiser Catches moles and no one has figured out how! Jacob gets to eat the leftover hotdogs from the clubhouse! Boerne most loves breakfast with the crew!

Lucky indeed is a Golf Course Dog.

Olympic Gold

Have you ever seen, held, or worn an Olympic Gold Medal? I have!

In the fall of 2009, my wife Cathy and I moved back to Overland Park Kansas from Hutchinson. My fun and amazing short time (2 ½ years) as General Manager at Prairie Dunes was now history.

I had set clear cut goals for the next chapter of my career. At 60 years old, I had a bit of an epiphany and was motivated and excited about what might be ahead.

I wrote a strategic business plan for the Midwest PGA Section, outlining a program to teach Elementary and Middle School Physical Education teachers, to teach golf in schools. Working closely with the Section PGA and the folks at SNAG (Starting New at Golf) we implemented the "SNAG in School" program.

I was asked and agreed to serve on two not for profit Boards. The Midwest PGA Section Foundation and the Kansas Golf Foundation. Both outstanding organizations, that do great things, have outstanding leadership, and have been fun to work with.

With a lot of patience and effort, after being closed for three years, the Twin Oaks Golf Complex in Eudora Kansas was reopened. The complex has a twenty-acre range, nine-hole, par 3 "Pitch and Putt" course, clubhouse, and a six-hole "Wee Links." Golf instruction has been and is the focus at Twin Oaks.

Shortly after reopening Twin Oaks, I was asked if I would like to teach, University of Kansas golf class (HESE 108). Since the University is just 4 miles away in Lawrence, I enthusiastically said "Yes" and have been teaching the course ever since. This class is 16 sessions, meets twice a week for 90 minutes and the students receive one-hour credit.

HESE 108 is one of my favorite things to be a part of. The Graduate assistants are fantastic, the 25-30 students have a wide range of experience, and at the end of the semester write and submit a Reflection essay. These kids are impressive! The Class covers, Golf history, rules, famous courses, recommended golf books/ movies, golf vocabulary, golf etiquette, instruction, practice, play, golf stories, and more.

The KU undergrads, male and female, have a wide variety of majors. We have future engineers, doctors, accountants, teachers, business majors, and more. There are also NCAA Division 1 athletes from all sports.

A few years back, in class, I had an athlete that was a Shot-putter. Mason Finley 6'8" weighed 350 pounds. Competing in China, Mason had set the world record for the Shot. Unfortunately, his record was broken an hour or so later. Mason our gentle giant ended up with the Bronze Medal!

Born in 1990, in Jonesboro Arkansas, Kyle Clemons came to Kansas from Rowlett High School in Garland Texas. Kyle is a track and field sprinter and a good one! He can fly and the 4 X 400 meter is his race. Kyle won Gold in the 2014 and 2016 World Indoor Championship. He won Bronze In the 400-meter individual at the 2015 Pan America games in Toronto. Also, in 2015 Clemons won Gold at the World Championships in Beijing.

Kyle's senior year, 2016, he took the Spring semester off! He needed to train for

Kyle Clemons

the 2016 Rio de Janeiro Summer Olympics. The training paid off as he ran the second leg of the 4 X 400 and the United States won.

Back to KU, Clemons needed one credit hour to graduate and decided to take HESE 108 with Professor Jeff. Kyle passed, is a Kansas Graduate, and hopefully will pursue golf as a hobby.

Not long after that class was completed, I was in a muddy hole repairing an irrigation leak. Cathy says: "Jeff, who is that?" Effortlessly sprinting our direction with a beaming smile was Kyle Clemons, coming to show us his Olympic Gold Medal.

Wow! It is a joy to teach the KU golf class!

ACKNOWLEDGMENTS

I have so enjoyed reflecting and writing about some of the many experiences I have lived on this wonderful journey. I am so thankful for all the folks that have positively impacted my life. It would be impossible to list these unbelievable individuals from all walks of life. Please know how appreciative I am!

I do want to acknowledge my three mentors:

Mike Krak

The "Pro's" Pro, Mike was and still is my hero! He was the near picture-perfect golf professional! Mike could play, a fantastic teacher, businessman and was so respected by his peers.

Mike gave this young inexperienced man, right out of the US Navy, a chance. I will always appreciate his genuine trust in me and his teaching me all the fundamentals needed to be a success in the golf business. I'm sure I was annoying at times, but he always was there.

I love and miss him!

Lou Miller

I have never met anyone quite like Lou Miller! Lou's "People" skills are unbelievable! He can uplift, encourage, and put a smile on your face. Lou empowers the people he works with and believes in their dreams.

I can't imagine a better leader, coach, friend, motivator, or more enthusiastic individual. I am grateful Lou had the confidence in me and allowed me to do a job and do other things that today seem beyond belief. I am so thankful for the opportunities granted to me by Lou.

Roy Pace

I knew of Roy when I was in high school and read in our local paper of his great playing success. I admired and followed RP's career on tour and later got to know him when he would come to Wee Burn before playing the Westchester or Hartford tour stops.

My time with Roy was priceless! Roy lives to teach and promote golf. His passion for junior golf is contagious and has played a gigantic part in my recent career. There were not many things more fun than playing with and watching Roy manage his golf game.

I experienced and got to work with Roy as he seamlessly transitioned from the PGA tour to Head Golf Professional. I will always appreciate Roy and will cherish the times we worked together.

Summary

My three mentors were all very different and yet have so much in common. These gentlemen as role models are as good as it gets!

These faithful men are all great husbands, fantastic dads, loyal, and professional in all ways.

Talented, consistent, confident, always teaching they allowed you to be creative and to do your job.

To the spouses: Susan Krak, Kay Miller, and Sandy Pace thank you for sharing your men with all of us!